African American Middle-Income Parents

How Are They Involved in Their Children's Literacy Development?

By

Ethel Swindell Robinson, Ph.D.

INFORMATION AGE PUBLISHING, INC.

Charlotte, NC • www.infoagepub.com

Library of Congress Cataloging-in-Publication Data

Robinson, Ethel Swindell.
  African American middle-income parents : how are they involved in their
children's literacy development? / by Ethel Swindell Robinson.
      p. cm. – (Language, literacy, and learning)
  Includes bibliographical references.
  ISBN-13: 978-1-59311-829-7 (pbk.)
  ISBN-13: 978-1-59311-830-3 (hardcover)
  1. African American children–Education. 2. Education–Parent
participation–United States–Case studies. 3. Reading–Parent
participation–United States–Case studies. I. Title.
  LC2778.L34R63 2007
  371.829'96073–dc22

                                                                        2007027014

CONTENTS

Foreword ix
Alfred W. Tatum, Ph.D.

Acknowledgments xi

1   Introduction: Middle-Income Images and Perceptions 1

2   Child's Literacy Learning: Like a Brick Wall Keeping Her
     on Task 13

3   Creating Positive Involvement Roles: Embracing Advocacy 21

4   Religion: The Umbrella for Parental Perceptions
     of Involvement 29

5   Involvement Roles: Not Fifty–Fifty 37

6   Involvement and Socialization Practices for Self-Sufficiency 47

7   Perceptions of Involvement and Micromanaging
     a Child's Education 57

8   A Parental Literacy Dilemma 65

9   Uncovering the Key Meaning of Parental Involvement 75

Conclusion 85

References 87

About the Author 91

FOREWORD

Several years ago, when my son was in the first grade, I was "called" to act on his behalf and on the behalf of other African American students because of an instructional activity that was part of the first-grade curriculum. The students were studying the origins of their classmates and constructing passports to chart their journeys to these different places— Greece, Ireland, Italy, China, Mexico, and *Kwanzaa*. As an African American middle-income parent, I immediately became concerned, because it was intimated that Kwanzaa was a place of origin, not a celebration envisioned in the late 1960s that emphasizes seven principles for the betterment of African Americans. Sadly, I found out that this same activity was four years old and had never been questioned.

Part of the problem I assessed was the relatively few numbers of African American students in the moderate- to high-income school district. Teachers had very minimal experience interacting with African American parents and had little knowledge about the expectations the parents held for their children. Therefore, the intent to honor the identity of African American students, although honorable, was woefully inadequate and misguided. While the first-grade students enjoyed the activity and failed to recognize the omission of the origin of their African American peers, this created a real tension for me as an African American parent.

This incident and several other culturally-entrenched incidents caused me to strike a delicate balance when communicating with the teachers. My son is a cultural being, but as a seven-year-old, was more interested in having a wonderful school year without the spoils of culture. Developmentally, he shared the same child-like qualities imported to class by the other students.

The intersection of culture, income, and schooling leads to many challenging questions. Which students' identities are of most worth? How can parents advocate for students' cultural identities and their academic identities that may have little to do with their cultural characteristics? How do

African American Middle-Income Parents, pages ix–x
Copyright © 2007 by Information Age Publishing

African American parents who are increasingly becoming middle-income communicate with primary teachers who are disproportionately White and female to share their desire to have their children's cultural characteristics acknowledged without reducing their children to "culture only?" How can parents and teachers reconcile differing belief systems about culture, language, and schooling without using children as pawns in these discussions?

To date, there is very little research that provides answers to the questions identified above. Fortunately, Ethel Robinson, has informed us that the role of middle-income African American parents' involvement during the primary years of their children's education is too important to ignore. She begins to unpack some to the dilemmas middle-income African American parents face as they move forward to provide the best educational opportunities for their children. This dilemma is couched in a national dilemma.

While schools have become increasingly diverse, many communities have not. Many middle-income communities still have a small relative share of African American families. This means, that in these communities, African American students from middle-income homes still constitute a small percentage of their school's population. This provides fewer opportunities for interaction between teachers in these schools and African American parents. With increased interactions, heightened understandings, and effective communication, we learn how teachers and African American middle-income parents are best able to protect the educational rights of all children. This text moves us in that direction.

—**Alfred W. Tatum, Ph.D.**
Northern Illinois University

ACKNOWLEDGMENTS

First, as always, I give glory, honor, and thanks to my Lord and Savior, Jesus Christ, for making it possible for me to write this book. Many thanks are extended to my sorority sisters and friends far and near, who believed in my lofty goal of becoming an author.

I am genuinely grateful to my professors for their assistance and guidance over the years. To Dr. Susan Hynds, for her insightful comments and suggestions on drafts of the manuscript—you continue to inspire me; and to Dr. Donald Leu, for your encouragement in absentia. A special thanks to the late Dr. Peter B. Mosenthal, for his enormous support. I miss you!

Appreciation is extended to Dr. Patricia Ruggiano Schmidt for giving me the first chance to write, and her belief and confidence in my capabilities; and to Dr. Alfred Tatum for writing the foreword. I would like to also thank Mrs. Mary McCurty and Dr. Mary Rucker for their editing expertise. Special thanks and appreciation to Dr. Cherlyn A. Johnson for her prayers, friendship, and encouragement.

Much gratitude is given to Mrs. Darlene Williams, Mrs. Jean Phillips, and Mrs. Sonya S. Hines for their support and for listening to my ideas, while I labored over mounds of papers and diskettes, instead of going shopping with them.

Heartfelt thanks to Pastor and Mrs. Milton Kornegay, for their support, and to the Central Baptist Church congregation for their unceasing prayers. I especially appreciate the technological support from Mrs. Carolon Dunlap.

This book could not have been written without the cooperation of the families who opened their homes and shared perceptions of their parental involvement practices. I am indebted to you for your willingness to be a part of this little-understood topic. I love each and every one of you. May God add a blessing to your lives.

Finally, I express my sincerest gratefulness to my son, his wife, my two grandchildren, and to all of my relatives. I adore and love you all.

CHAPTER 1

INTRODUCTION

Middle-Income Images and Perceptions

You have probably seen families like those you are about to meet, at least once in your lifetime. You may have seen them while they grocery shopped for their families before rushing off to a Parent Teacher Organization meeting. You may have seen them in church with their children, dressed in their Sunday best. You may have seen them as they visit their children's schools to express satisfaction or dissatisfaction with a teacher or a school policy, or to report an incident involving the inequitable treatment of a first-grade child.

You may have heard them in beauty/barber shops talking about setting expectations for their children or searching for the best teacher at a particular school. Their goals are to give their children a good education, so that they can be enrolled in one of America's best colleges. They may have been heard bragging about how they craft their involvement roles and design strategies to keep the lines of communication open, thus bridging the gap between home and school. Perhaps you have even heard them talk about their involvement with literacy learning, computers, homework, and long-term projects.

Who are these families? They may be middle-income African Americans with professional and blue-collar backgrounds who have children enrolled in first-grade classrooms. These middle-income African American parents belong to Generation X. Generation X is defined as the generation following the Baby Boomers. Individuals born between 1964 and 1979, fit into

African American Middle-Income Parents, pages 1–11
Copyright © 2007 by Information Age Publishing
All rights of reproduction in any form reserved.

the Generation X group (Coupland, 1991). At the time of the study, the age range of the parents was 35–37 years. They were gainfully employed and had the money, time, and resources to fully participate in their children's education and schooling. They had the latest technology in their homes, and their children were immersed in books and other print-rich materials. These Generation Xers are the children of the Baby Boomers, and unlike their parents, they grew up during the age of PCs, the Internet, email, and skateboards. They have the disposable income to purchase the necessary materials and supplies for their children. Consequently, these Generation X parents make every attempt to ensure their children's welfare in the school environment. They believe that because of the success they had economically, they are responsible for securing the best opportunities available to enable their children to succeed academically. Most of all, the value these parents place on education and their aspirations for their children's future economic success contribute to their perceptions and practices as they relate to their involvement with their children's schooling.

These middle-income families are not the people you see on the front page of the daily newspaper portraying the plight of African American parents in schools today. According to popular media's portrayal of the African American household, the typical family is one, which spends little time helping their children with literacy skills, thus placing them at a disadvantage even before preschool. The media also describes low-income and single-parent families as having academically, developmentally delayed children who have been labeled and placed in special education classes by the end of first-grade (Peters, 1981).

The middle-income families that you will meet in this book are just the opposite of the so-called dysfunctional families described above. In reality, in these families, both spouses are equally engaged at home, in the school, and the community. They are involved parents, they have control over their children's education, and they try to make a difference in their children's schooling.

Middle- and upper-middle-class African American families are seldom mentioned in the news. The popular media and the research community tend to view African American families as monolithic, regardless of income or social class. According to Cose (1999), more Blacks are entering the realm of the privileged. Yet, the media tends to overlook the fact that the "middle class" is a growing population. An article in *The Washington Post* clearly expressed that the segment of Black families earning $75,000 to $99,999, for example, grew almost four times between 1967 and 2003, increasing to 7 percent of the Black population. In comparison, White families in that income range just doubled, to 11.5 percent (Klein, 2004). In 1999, the Census Bureau revealed that salaries of middle- and upper-middle-class African Americans were on the rise. Salaries for African Americans ranged from a high of $75,000–$100,000 per family, to a low of $30,000–$35,000 per family (American Fact Finder U.S. Census Bureau Website, 1999).

Despite the growth of the Black middle class, we have little research on how this growing population participates in their children's education. The scarcity of literature on this group is apparent when vast amounts of scholarly studies are found on low-income African Americans and European middle-class families' involvement. As Robinson (1999) and Scanzoni (1971) have revealed, few studies have been conducted on middle-income African American parents' perceptions and practices as they relate to those parents' involvement with their first-grade children's schooling. This book was undertaken to address this gap.

The next section of this chapter offers background information on previous parent involvement literature. I first review the literature on the role of parental involvement in children's learning and achievement. Second, I present psychological and other variables that have influenced parents' involvement in schools. Third, I discuss the literature regarding how parents craft involvement roles. Last, I summarize the sparse literature on middle-income African American families, an under-represented group.

LOOKING BACK: THE LITERATURE ON PARENTAL INVOLVEMENT

Scholarly and public interest in parental involvement is not a new phenomenon. Researchers in early childhood education have long argued that parents' involvement in their children's education is essential for future success (Bronfenbrenner 1974; Comer, 1986, 1988, 1991; Galper, Wigfield, & Seefeldt, 1997; Henderson, 1987; Seefeldt, Denton, Galper, & Younoszia, 1998). Recently, with increased emphasis on children's early literacy development (National Institute of Health and Human Development, 2000), and improved reading in schools (Sadoski & Willson, 2006), school officials and policy makers have called for more parental involvement, especially from low-income African American families, families of color, and parents of first-grade children. More recently, policy makers have focused attention on the *No Child Left Behind Act* (2002), in an effort to ensure that every child can read at grade level or above not later than the end of third grade. As the following section will demonstrate, some previous research has been rather generic, focusing on parental involvement independent of race.

One of the longitudinal intervention studies on the effects of parents' involvement on children's learning was conducted with a group of disadvantaged preschoolers (Bronfenbrenner 1974). In this study, Bronfenbrenner assessed several intervention programs, and concluded that preschoolers attending these programs showed higher and longer lasting IQ gains if their mothers were active participants in their learning. The program that drew the most publicity was the 2-year intervention program whereby tutors visited homes twice weekly and demonstrated the use of learning kits to parents and children.

Parental involvement has also been linked to student achievement (Baumann & Thomas, 1999; Comer, 1988; Epstein, 1991; Henderson, 1987; Henderson & Berla, 1994; Taylor & Dorsey-Gaines, 1988). For instance, Comer (1986, 1988) designed a program to enhance communication and involvement between low-income, poor Black parents and school personnel. Because of their involvement in this program as decision makers, paid paraprofessionals, and volunteers, parents' participation in classrooms increased and their children's test scores rose (Comer & Haynes, 1991). Epstein (1991) found that when low-income parents know that schools want them involved they take an active role in their children's education and schooling.

The importance of parents' participation in children's schooling has been well documented (Comer, 1988; Comer & Haynes, 1991; Dauber & Epstein, 1993; Edwards, 1995, 2005; Henderson, 1987; Hoover-Dempsey & Sandler, 1997; Lightfoot, 1978; Schmidt, 2005). In their report, *The Evidence Continues to Grow,* Henderson and Berla (1994) summarized 49 research studies which demonstrated some of the major benefits that occur when parents are involved. They concluded that when parents are involved in their children's education, children do better in school and they attend better schools. As Hoover-Dempsey and Sandler (1997) have noted, "across a range of studies, there has emerged a strong conclusion that parental involvement in child and adolescent education generally benefits children's learning and school success" (p. 3).

Much previous scholarship excludes middle-class African American families. According to Coner-Edwards and Spurlock (1988), "Middle-class Blacks are often omitted from discussions of Black people, Black communities, and inner city Blacks; although middle-class Blacks exist among all three" (p. v). Previous studies, however, of African American families have tended to focus on low-income populations (Baumann & Thomas, 1999; Edwards, 1995, 2004; Heath, 1983; Lightfoot, 1978; Overstreet, Devine, Bevans, & Efreom, 2005; Taylor & Dorsey-Gaines, 1988). Thus, our professional and public perceptions of parental involvement among African American families are based on a relatively small and restricted sample. Perhaps, unwittingly, researchers and policy makers have overlooked the fact that in-group differences exist among African American families and have perpetuated the notion that these families are homogeneous and uninvolved with their children's education. These statements are far from the truth. The greatest sign of this kind of deformation was shown when Moynihan (1965) examined the 1960 National Census data and discovered that nearly a quarter of the homes were matriarchal. He argued that the structure of Black families was dysfunctional, parents showed little interest or involvement in their children's education, and that the Black family was responsible for its own demise. As stated by Peters (1981), studies conducted on African American families tend to focus on the involvement roles of low-income malfunctioning families. Seemingly, some scholars have focused exclusively on this low-income group, thus treating race as a monolithic variable and, perpetuating the notion that all African Americans are uninvolved with their children's schooling.

VARIABLES THAT INFLUENCE PARENTAL INVOLVEMENT

Other studies have focused on factors that influence the degree of parental involvement in children's schooling. It has been shown that family status variables (i.e., cultural beliefs, income, race, ethnicity, efficacy beliefs, education, and marital status) predict parents' involvement (Eccles & Harold, 1993; Fine, 1993; Galper et al., 1997; Seefeldt et al., 1998).

In a short summary of the literature on parent involvement, Eccles and Harold (1993) reported that parents with higher levels of education were more involved in school and at home than parents who have less education. Dauber and Epstein (1993) surveyed 2,317 economically disadvantaged parents to determine what influenced their school involvement. It was concluded that parents' education strongly predicted their level of involvement at school.

However, some studies have debunked the stereotypical idea that less-educated, low-income African American parents were uninvolved in their children's schooling (Baumann & Thomas, 1999; Taylor & Dorsey-Gaines, 1988). For instance, Baumann and Thomas' (1999) case study demonstrated how two researchers, a teacher and a parent, worked together for one year to explore their beliefs about teaching and how literacy learning developed in a low-income family. Baumann and Thomas concluded that contrary to social biases and beliefs, single parents in poor Black families did care about their children's education and had strong connections with the school. Likewise, Taylor and Dorsey-Gaines (1988) conducted an ethnographic study with four poor African American families whose children were enrolled in first-grade. They were learning to read and write; and their homes were immersed with books and various print materials. The researchers concluded that even though these parents lived in the inner city, were poor, and less educated, they were highly involved in their children's education.

Some studies have revealed that parents with strong self-efficacy beliefs were able to construct involvement roles for themselves and were more involved than parents with a low sense of efficacy (Bandura, Barbaranelli, Caprara, & Pastorelli, 1996; Bandura, 1997; Galper et al., 1997; Seefeldt et al., 1998). For example, Galper et al. (1997) examined a group of 124 ethnically diverse parents' beliefs (i.e., Hispanic, African American, and Asian subgroups) about their former Head Start children's abilities and values, as well as their expectations for the children's future success in school during the children's kindergarten year. Galper et al. concluded that these parents were positive about their children's future and school-related abilities. In a similar study, Seefeldt et al. (1998) surveyed and interviewed 253 parents from a number of races and ethnicities such as Asian, African American, Hispanic, and European American. All parents had children who were enrolled in the Head Start program. The parents were investigated concerning self-efficacy beliefs and their level of involvement in their children's academic abilities at the end of kindergarten. Seefeldt et al. concluded that the parents' sense of efficacy belief was strong; they believed they could help their children and had the ability to exercise control over their education.

Among the many variables that have influenced parents' involvement in schools, income is believed to be a fairly stable predictor. Studies such as those by Fine (1993) on reform and restructuring of schools in three cities (i.e., Baltimore, Philadelphia, and Chicago) revealed that income/resources influenced the degree to which parents participated in the decision-making process and in their children's schooling. Fine concluded that most often, parents from middle- and upper-middle-class communities came to meetings with more resources and were more likely to become involved with their children's education than parents from low-income communities.

Lately, researchers have begun to examine different variables that may have predicted parents' involvement. For instance, Sheldon (2002) analyzed the degree to which parents socialized with other parents as a predictor of participation in children's schooling. Sheldon concluded that apart from parents' beliefs, social networks were drastically connected with levels of parental involvement.

Another significant study that discussed variables that predicted parental involvement was conducted by Overstreet, Devine, Bevans, and Efreom (2005); they examined 159 economically disadvantaged African American parents of elementary and middle school children to determine predictors of parental involvement within the school. Other factors such as demographics, parents' attitudes about education, and their perceptions of the school's receptivity to involvement were also explored. Overstreet et al.,

(2005), concluded that school receptivity was a significant predictor of parent–school contact for parents of elementary and middle school students.

To date, few studies have been conducted on middle-income African American families and the variables that predict their involvement in their children's education. Hence, the question remains as to how middle-income, African American parents perceive their involvement with their first-grade children's schooling and how those perceptions influence their reported practices.

IMPEDIMENTS TO AFRICAN AMERICAN PARENTAL INVOLVEMENT AND ROLE CONSTRUCTION

The need for parental involvement can be traced back as far as biblical scripture. For example, Proverbs 22:6 states, "Train up a child in the way he should go, and when he is old, he will not depart from it." However, over three decades ago, researchers argued that low-income African American families had little input in training their children and were not allowed to construct school involvement roles for themselves in their children's education (Lightfoot, 1978; Ogbu, 1977). Lightfoot used in-depth interviews to study how teachers perceived the role of parents in the elementary school setting and found that despite African American parents' pleas for empowerment, teachers refused to collaborate with them about their children's education. Consequently, conflict occurred as teachers and parents struggled to gain control over the children's education. Lightfoot concluded that middle-class White teachers did not want to have positive relationships with low-income Black parents. Similarly, in an ethnographic study, Ogbu (1977) interviewed and observed Black American parents and found that role construction was difficult for them due to school policies and procedures, such as racial stratification, low teacher expectations, and negative teacher–parent relationships. Parents believed that the inequality of opportunities caused Black children to fail. Ogbu (1977) concluded that low-income Black children believed that education was not a vehicle to social mobility and opportunity.

Although it was difficult for parents and teachers to work as partners in Black children's education years ago, federal and state laws such as the *Goals 2000: Educate America Act* empowers and encourages parents to participate in their children's education (U. S. department of Education, 1994). Studies such as those by Galper et al. 1997; and Seefeldt et al., 1998, have shown how Head Start, a federally funded program, encourages parents to take an active role in their children's education.

Some studies have shown that how parents viewed their roles in their children's education varied across parents (Reed, Jones, Walker, & Hoover-

Dempsey, 2000) and ethnic groups (Delgado-Gaitan, 1992; Espinosa, 1995). To improve the process of reaching out to parents, Espinosa (1995) presented seven strategies for obtaining and cheering Hispanic parents' involvement in Early Childhood programs. Espinosa reported that as a cultural practice, Hispanic parents did not choose a role for themselves in their children's education. They believed that education was the responsibility of schools.

In a different vein, Delgado-Gaitan (1992) observed and interviewed six working Mexican American families, as they spontaneously interacted with their children. Delgado-Gaitan studied parents' attitudes toward their children and the roles the families played in the socialization of their second graders. These parents gave their children the emotional and motivational support that caused them to enjoy reading. Delgado-Gaitan (1992) concluded that involvement in the home varied according to parents' education, materials in the home, socialization patterns, and knowledge of the school's expectations.

To further explore parental role construction, Dauber and Epstein (1993) surveyed 2,317 economically disadvantaged parents from an urban neighborhood and found that school practices designed to get parents involved encouraged their participation at school, in the home, and in the community. Hoover-Dempsey and Sandler's (1997) literature review, also noted that parents construct roles for themselves when they were welcome or received invitations to participate at school.

Most families want to create partnerships with their child's teachers to improve the child's academic success (Epstein, 1996). Glenn Paul (2000) agreed with Epstein, in that the reason to create partnerships is to help children succeed in school and succeed in life. Consequently, to implement the notion of partnerships, researcher Epstein (1996) created a framework of five types of involvement designed for school districts and states to develop and maintain partnership programs that improved student success. The framework included: parenting, communication, volunteering, decision making, and collaborating with the community. It should be noted however, that training for parents and all educators is a necessity if parents and teachers are to work together as partners. Among the five types of involvement, each was likely to lead to different results. Epstein (1996) concluded that parents' involvement at home and in the school was a major factor for increasing students' achievement.

Although previous studies have identified some of the barriers to impede low-income racially diverse parents' abilities to construct involvement roles, little is known about the manner in which middle-income, African American families craft involvement roles and deal with the obstructions that impede involvement. Because most literature has focused on low-income African American parents, the conclusions that mass media, some social scientists, teachers, and policy makers have drawn may be unrepresentative of African Americans as a whole. This is a particular concern in light of the growing middle-income African American population in the United States (Attewell, Lavin, Domina, & Levey, 2004; Masci, 1998).

RESEARCH ON MIDDLE-INCOME
AFRICAN AMERICAN PARENTAL INVOLVEMENT

As noted above, the parent involvement literature based on middle-income African American families is sparse. In reviewing the literature, only two studies were identified that focused on middle-income African American parents' perceptions of involvement with their primary children's education and schooling (Robinson, 1999; Scanzoni, 1971). Using qualitative research methods, Robinson (1999) interviewed 19 middle-income African American families about their perceptions of participation in their primary children's literacy learning in the home, not at school per se. Robinson concluded that parental beliefs about their children's academic achievement needed to be shared with teachers and that literacy learning in one environment ultimately supported learning in the other.

In contrast, in an ex post facto, quasi-three generation longitudinal study, Scanzoni (1971) surveyed adolescent offsprings of 400 Black parents above the poverty level by exploring their past life cycle as adolescents and present involvement with their second-grade children's education. Scanzoni (1971) asked the offspring generation how they perceived their parents' involvement, and orientation toward achievement and employment. Scanzoni concluded that both generations of nonpoor Black families were involved with their children's education and stressed upward mobility and economic success through "anticipatory socialization," a method of counseling and an example used by Black parents to help their children get ahead in life. Lastly, he suggested that when compared with White families at the same social class levels, economic opportunities were possible for Black families if the playing field was level (p. 265).

Given that few studies to date have been specifically conducted on the nature of middle-income African American parents' perceptions of involvement and reported practices with their first-grade children's education, I chose to make this topic the purpose of my study.

INVESTIGATING THE PARENTS' LIFE-WORLD

My case study of eight intact middle-income, African American families investigated their perceptions of the kinds of involvement and practices in which they engaged with their first-grade children's education (Stake 1995, 2000). The interviews were conducted in a manner reflective of the phenomenological perspective, because it allowed me to better understand the parents' perceptions of their involvement in their life-world (c.f. Schutz, 1970; Seidman, 1998).

I interviewed parents in their homes in dyads for one hour twice monthly over the course of a year to ascertain their involvement in all aspects of home, school, and community activities. Ultimately, I collected over 500 pages of transcribed data. To gather the data, I used semistructured, in-depth, life-world interviews (Kvale, 1996). Following the traditions of Bogdan and Biklen (1998), the interviews were audio taped, and analytic memos were written to help maintain focus on emerging themes. After the interviews were transcribed, data were analyzed to see how parents' perceptions of involvement practices with their children differed among the eight families (Yin, 1994). Data analysis occurred concurrently with data collection. Finally, during analysis and coding of data, two major traditional categories emerged: parents' perceptions of their involvement practices at home, and parents' perceptions of their involvement practices at school. Through further analysis of data, five thematic topics were identified for each category. These themes described how most parents perceived their involvement practices with the child's education "at home" as advocates, promoters of learning, providers of a good education, initiators of goals and expectations, and crafters of equal involvement roles. Similarly, they talked about their perceptions of involvement practices "at school," in themes such as, monitoring schools' routines, schooling satisfaction, fostering communication, bridging home and school, and participating in parent/teacher organizations (PTOs). In addition, some parents discussed their involvement practices with their children in the church and in the community. Traditionally, the home and school contexts are where parental involvement takes place. Recently, however, involvement in the community has been added to the parental involvement landscape.

As I interviewed the families, I was aware of potential biases from my previous background as an early childhood educator, having taught in the Bellport school system before becoming an administrator. I tried to forget my biases and assumptions about parental involvement. I did not want them to interfere with the stories the families conveyed about their involvement and practices with their first-grade children's education. Knowing that I was an insider, but an outsider to them, I was concerned that it might be difficult getting the parents to respond. As I gained the families' confidence and trust, they became open and willing to talk.

SUMMARY OF THE PARENT INVOLVEMENT LITERATURE

The literature surveyed in this chapter revealed that parental involvement is an important factor in enhancing students' academic achievement and for their success later in life (Allington & Cunningham, 2002; Bronfenbrenner, 1974; Comer, 1986; Henderson, 1987, 1994; H. P. McAdoo, 1997; U.S. Department of Education, 1994). Issues of parental involvement are complicated among African-American families. However, since schools are overwhelmingly staffed with European American teachers and administrators, studies of low-income African-American families have demonstrated that although parents valued education, teachers tended to undervalue and discourage parental participation (Lightfoot, 1978; Ogbu, 1977, 1995). Despite such discouragement, parents with strong self-efficacy beliefs about children's learning and future success are able to construct important roles for themselves (Galper et al., 1997; Seefeldt et al., 1998). In addition, parents' social networks influence parents at home and at school (Sheldon, 2002) and school receptivity is found to be a strong predictor of school involvement (Overstreet et. al., 2005).

Although there are studies contributing to our understanding of low-income parents of diverse races and ethnicities, it is unclear what middle-income African American families believe about their roles in their children's future school success. Little research (Scanzoni, 1971; Robinson, 1999) on middle-income African American parents exists despite a growing middle-class African American population in the United States (Masci, 1998; Cose, 1993, 1999; Klein, 2004; Drum Major Institute, 2004). Clearly, more research is needed on this growing class of middle-income African American parents' and their perceptions of involvement with their first-grade children's education. This qualitative, collective case study was conducted to fill a significant void in the parent involvement literature. Throughout the following eight chapters, parents discuss their perceptions of involvement and reported practices in which they engaged, regarding their first-grade children's education.

CHAPTER 2

CHILD'S LITERACY LEARNING

Like a Brick Wall Keeping Her on Task

THE HARVEY FAMILY

I met Tommy and Joyce Harvey through the president of the local chapter of Jack and Jill, Inc., a family organization which evolved from a group founded in Philadelphia in 1939, to provide for their children when segregation limited Black's opportunities. The purpose of Jack and Jill is to support Black families and stimulate the growth and development of children by providing constructive educational, cultural, civic, recreational, and social programs to enrich their lives. Joyce was a member of this prestigious organization and her daughter Allison was in the middle group that consisted of children 7–8 years of age.

Tommy and Joyce Harvey had been married for 10 years. Tommy, a native Bellportian, was the first in his family to graduate from college. He had an Associates of Arts and Science degree in Business Administration and was continuing his education part-time, while working as an inspector with the fire department. Mrs. Harvey was not a college graduate, but had taken some computer and professional growth courses. She had worked for the same chemical company since high school and proudly stated, "I worked my way up the career ladder and am now in middle management." The Harvey's were members of the Presbyterian church where Tommy had been a member all of his life. The family was active in the church and attended services every Sunday.

African American Middle-Income Parents, pages 13–20

In a series of dialogues, Tommy and Joyce discussed their perceptions of their involvement and practices with their first-grade daughter Allison's education in the home, the school, and in the community.

Normally, parents in the city of Bellport chose to enroll their children in one of several types of schools (i.e., public, parochial, private, and home schooling). The Harvey's chose to send their daughter, Allison, to a small Catholic school.

Catholic School: Absolutely!

Tommy and Joyce recounted their experiences of choosing a school for Allison. When she was a toddler, they placed her name on a waiting list for enrollment at St. Agatha's, a small Catholic School near their house. That was their choice, because Tommy had attended parochial schools throughout his elementary and high school education. Joyce attended public schools, but agreed to send Allison to St. Agatha's. She said, "I was afraid to send my baby girl to a public school."

Reminiscing about his childhood days, Tommy proudly said, "All of my siblings attended Catholic schools." He conveyed that both of his parents worked. They used their salaries to send the children to St. Bernadette and St. Agnes, two Catholic schools on the west side of Bellport. According to Tommy, financially, it wasn't easy for his parents to send all of the children to parochial schools, but they made the sacrifice, because they wanted the best education for their children. He further stated,

> We were not a rich family, but with six children back in the fifties, my parents were really struggling. Like my parents, we want our daughter to get the best education. Finances are not a major struggle for us and, the Catholic school is absolutely our choice!

Parental Involvement and Literacy Learning

At age five, Allison entered kindergarten at St. Agatha's Catholic School. Immediately, her parents began their involvement with the school by monitoring their daughter's academic activities, especially homework assignments, and participating in the PTA. They were in contact with Ms. Booker, the kindergarten teacher, and welcomed her input regarding Allison's academic growth. Early on, Ms. Booker noticed that Allison was not focusing on her schoolwork. So, one day, when Mr. Harvey took his daughter to school, Ms. Booker told him about Allison's off-task behavior. Promptly, upon arrival at home, Tommy told Joyce what the teacher had said about their daughter's daydreaming habits during class time. They, too, had noticed that Allison was not attentive while studying at home.

Allison's behavior intensified during her first-grade year. She constantly left her seat and talked with her classmates about independent seatwork assignments instead of speaking with her teacher. Since Allison was not completing these assignments during the school day, they were sent home in her backpack. Therefore, Allison had to not only complete the seatwork, but also, the homework assignments. Consequently, Allison's parents helped her with homework for over an hour every evening. They became very concerned and reprimanded their daughter for not remaining on task during the school day. Her off-task behaviors frustrated the parents and the first-grade teacher. Additionally, Allison had not mastered the phonics in her beginning reading program. Mr. Harvey commented,

> It was like getting through a brick wall keeping her on task. I used the metaphor, *it was like a brick wall keeping her on task,* to describe Allison's strong willed behavior as it related to her ability to remain focused and capable of correcting her own mistakes.

Mr. Harvey struck at the heart of the matter when he said:

> Realizing that Allison had problems remaining on task, I drew my own theory on the approaches she needed to learn effectively. Knowing her learning style, and different strategies to use when assisting her, learning for her could be easier. Perhaps, if she learned a variety of ways to attack a problem, whether it is math, spelling, or reading, she would do better academically.

Relative to reading and phonics, Allison continued to need assistance. Mrs. Gibson sent home phonics worksheets for Allison to complete under the tutelage of the parents. One day, Mrs. Gibson called Joyce about the problem Allison had with vowel sounds. Joyce asked the teacher, "Did you ever think that maybe Allison needs extra help from you or someone at the school?" Joyce further stated,

> Now, the school has hired a specially-trained reading teacher to provide reading support for children at each grade level, especially beginning readers who are struggling with phonics. I became more concerned each time I tried to teach Allison vowel sounds. I know that our daughter needs more help with vowels than either of us can give her. I am thankful that the school has hired a special reading teacher.

At our next meeting, Allison's literacy learning was the main topic of discussion. To begin the conversation, the parents were asked if Allison's reading had improved. Mr. Harvey answered the question immediately, "She is getting better. She needs to keep working on it though. Last night, she read three books." He continued to explain his frustration with his daughter.

> She is more motivated to do her work. However, she likes to follow others.... We still have to constantly remind her to stay on task, but I have seen tremendous improvement in reading.

Joyce interjected,

> I am working with her on following rules, like staying in her seat, especially when the teacher is teaching; she must respect the teacher.

In relation to teaching the child respect for the teacher, Mrs. Harvey stated that it was their responsibility to encourage their daughter to learn and become academically successfully. Furthermore, she said that learning was what Allison did on a daily basis. It encompassed all of her experiences. Mr. Harvey continued the conversation.

> We encourage Allison's learning by reading to her, taking her to the library, to church, and to cultural events. Not everything is reading, writing, and arithmetic; she will have to learn other things to survive on her own. Even when she is at ballet class, playing T-ball, rehearsing for the church choir, camping, or exploring cooking, she is learning. School learning is not the only form of education.

Moreover, according to Tommy, their desires and aspirations for Allison were expressed in terms of motivating and improving her overall school behavior (i.e., staying on task and obeying school protocol).

School Administrator

Allison had been at St. Agatha's Catholic school for two years, and her parents had not mentioned Sister Pat, the principal of the school. For that reason, I queried them about their satisfaction with the school's administrator. Tommy did not comment on the question. Joyce expressed her dissatisfaction with Sister Pat. She stated,

> I believe Sister Pat is not well informed in the latest leadership skills. What I mean by that is, I think she has lost some of the skills needed to run a school. She doesn't know what kids need today. I believe she is operating from past perspectives. Not in a bad way, because the kids still listen to her. In this diverse society, I think the school should enroll more minority students and hire some African American teachers.

CRAFTING DOABLE INVOLVEMENT
ROLES IN THREE CONTEXTS

Traditionally, parental involvement has resembled a three-legged stool. It consists of involvement in three contexts, the home, at school, and in the community. Tommy and Joyce reported that they were involved in all of these contexts.

The Harvey's perceptions of home involvement and practices consisted of helping Allison with homework assignments, literacy learning, and other related tasks. For instance, one Saturday Tommy revealed an interesting story about his involvement with Allison in the area of physical development. To enhance Allison's large motor skills, he purchased roller blades and taught her to skate. This activity required supervision, so Tommy needed to participate as well. Therefore, he purchased a pair of roller blades for himself and skated along with his daughter. He was happy to report this experience and said, "I had just as much fun as my daughter!"

On another visit with this family, Joyce greeted me at the door with a big smile. Tommy, though, seemed rather tired. It was later revealed that he had worked the night before and had not gotten enough sleep. Nevertheless, he participated in the conversation relative to school involvement and the Parent Teacher Association (PTA).

During the interview, Tommy and Joyce recounted the involvement and practices in which they engaged with the school. One of the most striking features about this meeting was the parents' explanations of equal involvement in school activities. When the question about PTA was posed, Tommy perked up, leaned back in his chair, chuckled and spoke very positively about his volunteer experiences. Describing their PTA work, he explained,

> At the first Parent Teacher Association meeting, teachers post a list of activities, and parents volunteered for what they thought were their best talents. I signed the list to participate in the school picnic, field trips, and keeping the children safe while teachers attended monthly meetings. I also volunteered to make my daughter's costume for a holiday program.

Mrs. Harvey added,

> All of those activities were set up at the beginning of the school year. I have done four field trips this year, the science museum, the zoo, the pumpkin farm, and a camping trip. Later this year, I will watch students at lunchtime while teachers attend the teacher appreciation luncheon. I also coach T-ball after school.

In addition to volunteering and assisting with school activities, the Harveys found time to communicate with Allison's teacher and attend other school related programs.

According to Tommy and Joyce, they were active in most school activities; when they could not attend a particular function, Tommy's father accompanied Allison. If grandpa Harvey could not attend a school activity, one of Joyce's parents substituted. Joyce Harvey described a recent week at the school:

> We went to the educational fair yesterday. It was one of the major attractions of the year. We saw some of Allison's work that she had completed in class; just a few of her activities were exhibited. Nevertheless, we were pleased to see her work on display. Later we went to the gymnasium and saw the science fair projects that fifth and sixth grades were exhibiting. The *Spring Concert* was also held this week. Two nights out in one week is tiring, but we participate in these programs because it is our responsibility to know what goes on at the school.

After concluding the topic on school involvement, the Harveys revealed how they perceived their involvement in the community. Community involvement consisted of Allison's ballet lessons at Madam Whitaker's dance school, the church choir, and her T-ball games. In addition, Joyce accompanied Allison to monthly activities sponsored by the Jack and Jill children's group. Mrs. Harvey described a specific Jack and Jill cultural event:

> We took Allison to the gospel concert over the weekend, and she enjoyed it very much. It was a Black orchestra that came to Bellport. The gospel music was spiritually uplifting for all of us. Some of the words in the song reinforced what we teach Allison in the home. I think it is important for her to hear symphonic music and to know when a violin or a cello is being played. Each month, Allison's Jack and Jill group participate in a cultural event; I am involved in all Jack and Jill community activities.

SUMMARY: LIKE A BRICK WALL KEEPING HER ON TASK

In this chapter, I have presented evidence of the Harvey family's perceptions of their involvement and reported practices with the education and schooling of Allison in three contexts, the school, the home, and in the community. You have read the parents concerns about their daughter's reading development. Mrs. Harvey was adamant in her quest that St. Agatha's Catholic School provide Allison with more phonetic assistance. The parents sent her to a Catholic school because they believed she would receive a better education in that setting. They also crafted involvement roles in three contexts and implemented them in conjunction with busy work schedules and with the help of extended family members. In addition, they were members of the PTA, volunteered in school activities, and participated in yearly events.

MY PERSONAL REFLECTIONS

My personal connections relate to the Harvey's comments about choosing a school for their daughter, her literacy development, and about hiring more teachers of color. Their remarks bring to mind many similarities as I analyze my past experiences in order to fully connect with this family in their parental involvement roles relative to schooling choices, literacy, and the teacher selection process.

Choosing a School

As parents who had just relocated to Bellport in the late 1960s, we were faced with the task of selecting a school for Mitchell, our first-grade son. I can recall how ambivalent we became when we learned that he would be bussed to a school outside of our neighborhood. We had heard positive remarks about the Catholic school where I worked as a public school pre-kindergarten teacher. Therefore, we chose to enroll him at that school. It was convenient, and had an excellent academic program. We wanted a strict educational program for our son, because he was already reading. Like the Harvey's we wanted to provide the best education for him.

Literacy Development

I can recall the day my son learned to read. He read to us from a simple book consisting of word families written as funny stories. Several children in my preschool class had learned to read from that same book after using the moveable Montessori alphabets and becoming aware of letters and sounds. Like my son, the preschoolers learned quickly that sounds and letters went together to make words, and words and pictures were used to write easy to read stories.

Drawing on my own experience, as an early childhood educator, I have seen children who learn to read without knowing any phonics. Case in point, my granddaughter is just beginning to learn vowel sounds, yet she is reading. Some people, however, believe a child must know all of the vowels and consonants before learning to read. Some children learn to read by sight, but most seem to need some phonemic knowledge in order to help them become more successful readers.

Hiring Teachers of Color

I can remember reading an article in the *Daily Newspaper* that stated there were no African American teachers available for hire, even though administrators had attempted to recruit current college graduates. Like Mrs. Harvey, I too agree that parents should see more teachers and administrators of color in the schools. Lack of available teachers of color is a national problem. To get more personnel of color in school systems these institutions should nurture and prepare more teachers and administrators who are products of the local school system.

Just before retiring from my position as an administrator in the school system, I interviewed new teacher candidates. At that time, teachers of color were becoming sparse within the education arena. This was partially due to lack of recruitment and the fact that there were other fields with higher paying salaries that attracted this younger group of graduates. Parents, however, who feel that their children's school should hire more African American teachers should get involved, voice their concerns to the superintendent of schools, and become advocates for the cause.

CHAPTER 3

CREATING POSITIVE
INVOLVEMENT ROLES

Embracing Advocacy

THE KEYS FAMILY

Paul and Mary Keys lived on the east side of the city in an upscale neighbor-hood. From what was seen of their ranch style home, it was well furnished and beautifully decorated. The couple had been married for 10 years and described themselves as middle class parents. They were a blended family with two sons and a daughter. A blended family is the union between hus-band and wife with children from previous marriages (e.g., the Brady Bunch). Andrew, the focal child, attended the public school in their neigh-borhood. Their daughter was a freshman at Mazoo State University major-ing in business education. The older son, Joseph, was in middle school.

Paul Keys was the first one in his family to graduate from college with a Bachelor of Arts degree in engineering. He was employed as a mechanical engineer for a division of Packard Corporation. His parents instilled in him the importance of getting a good education. Mary, a banking reconcilia-tion clerk, was from Bellport. She had an Associates of Arts degree in Humanities from Bellport Community College. Additionally, she had an art business. Mary was a first generation college graduate. Her parents made every effort to see that their children completed high school and col-lege. Mr. and Mrs. Keys stated that they were a church-going family. Mary

African American Middle-Income Parents, pages 21–28
Copyright © 2007 by Information Age Publishing

sang in the choir and Paul was a member of the deacon board. Joseph was in the youth choir and served on the youth usher board. Andrew participated in the youth fellowship group.

The First Meeting

In the course of collecting background information about the family, they were reticent to speak with me. In order to encourage dialogue during the questioning process, an icebreaker was used. That is, I talked about my martial status, place of birth, siblings, and college education. The icebreaker freed the family to speak about themselves and Andrew, the focal child. It was pointed out that they had just bought a home on the east side of Bellport and shopped around for the best school for Andrew. They also revealed their educational backgrounds, employment, and socioeconomic status. When the meeting had ended, a time and date were set for the next meeting.

Making School Choices: Embracing Advocacy

During subsequent interviews, the family was more talkative. Mrs. Keys discussed the importance of choosing the best school for their son even if it meant transferring him to a school outside of the neighborhood. As she began to communicate with her neighbors, she was informed that there were outstanding teachers at the neighborhood school. One neighbor told them about Mrs. Boston who was her child's first-grade teacher. When Mary and Paul Keys registered Andrew for first-grade, they requested that teacher. With the principal's approval, Andrew's name was placed on Mrs. Boston's class list. Subsequently, they enrolled him in the neighborhood school, monitored his progress, and became involved in his education.

As the months unfolded, the parents discussed Andrew's progress in first-grade. Mrs. Keys talked about her son's early childhood years. When Andrew was three years old, he was diagnosed with a speech problem. The parents made the choice to send him to speech therapy. Mary Keys said she "was really kind of apprehensive about sending him to speech therapy." But, they believed that his speech impediment would cause problems later. Therefore, the couple thought it would be best to address the problem early on. After two years of speech therapy, his records were sealed. Mrs. Keys recounted,

> When Andrew was younger he couldn't say his own name. Now he talks too much. As far as his grades are concerned, he's doing excellent and is on level in reading. His report card is more like 5's and 4's; like A's and B's. So we're

really blessed and glad that we gave him the proper support as far as speech therapy is concerned. It hasn't hindered him thus far; he's moving forward. He enjoys reading and is very excited… Reading and math are two areas where he really excels and loves very much.

This family took an active role in choosing where to enroll the child in order to ensure a "good education."

PARENTAL INVOLVEMENT IN THE HOME

Perceptions of Setting Expectations and Receiving a Good Education

Several weeks later, when we met, Paul informed me of their expectations for Andrew. It was discovered that the parents expected Andrew to strive for excellence. Accordingly, Paul and Mary expressed immediate goals such as learning to read, to write, and to logically solve mathematical and other problems he might encounter in his daily life. Moreover, Mr. and Mrs. Keys wanted Andrew to be responsible, obedient, and become an independent thinker. Mr. Keys stated,

We expect Andrew to try as hard as he can… If he is trying to do his best and is obedient to authority, he is going to be all right. An additional expectation is that he becomes more independent and responsible for his own learning.

In agreement with her husband, Mrs. Keys reflected on how she expected her son to perform on a particular homework assignment.

Just before you came in, I was going over his homework writing assignment and had him rewrite it because his penmanship is beautiful, but he's writing his words too close together. I was just telling him that and explaining that he should just take the extra time and do it right.

Getting a Good Education

According to Paul Keys, to receive a good education and become successful in school and later on in life, Andrew needed structure and motivation. Paul explained what a good education meant to him.

Getting a good education means that when Andrew graduates from high school and college, he will be prepared to enter the workforce. More immediately it means getting the fundamental or basic skills at the elementary level that will help him complete high school and pursue a college major. He will need skills, structure, communication, and motivation to be successful in the workplace.

In an effort to learn about the parent's perceptions of involvement in the school, we addressed their contentment with the teacher.

Schooling Satisfaction

With respect to schooling satisfaction, Mary Keys stated that they were delighted to have Mrs. Boston as Andrew's first-grade teacher. Moreover, they were happy that they made the decision to request her as his teacher. Mary pointed out that Mrs. Boston was very cooperative, and a good listener. She explained,

> I don't know a whole lot about Mrs. Boston, but she was highly recommended. We wanted Andrew to have a firm teacher with structure, and one who would teach children. Some teachers are okay, but they're lacking in some areas. We can't complain about Mrs. Boston. I am hoping that we can get a teacher like her for second grade.

PARENTAL INVOLEMENT IN THE SCHOOL

Communicating With the Teacher

During the months ahead, communicating and establishing a positive relationship with the teacher were discussed with the couple. For instance, the family expressed their school involvement roles and reported how they collaborated with the teacher. Paul conveyed that he communicated with the teacher several days a week. In fact, he inquired about Andrew's progress in different areas of learning, particularly reading.

Mrs. Keys continued the conversation with a different perspective. She concurred that they talked with Mrs. Boston at school, but they could also communicate with her in informal settings as well. Mary Keys said,

> Basically, we communicate by going into the classroom, talking with the teacher, or calling her at home. Once I saw Mrs. Boston in the supermarket, and we discussed Andrew's progress. She gave me the impression that she's very proud of him. She is willing to work with us over the summer by giving us ideas that we can use to help prepare him for the second grade.

In relation to communicating with the school in general, Paul described the school's policy, as he perceived it:

Our son's school has the open door policy for parents. You can come any time, and they encourage the parents to come. So, I volunteer in his classroom, interact with his teacher and encourage him to do his best in the class. At the end of the school day, I always ask him, "How was your day in school?" Then I try to go through a short review of what he did in the class that day.

Establishing a Positive Partnership With the Teacher

With regard to establishing a positive relationship with Mrs. Boston, the Keys family said they had created an educational partnership with her earlier in the school year. In essence, Paul began volunteering in Mrs. Boston's classroom in September. Working nights provided him the luxury of being home during the day. Hence, he walked Andrew to school every day; rather than return home immediately, he remained in the classroom to assist Mrs. Boston. She relied on Paul to help her on a regular basis. Moreover, Paul volunteered so frequently, he did not have to schedule an appointment to communicate with Mrs. Boston about his son's progress. At the same time, he said he was constructing an educational partnership with the teacher and the school.

Constructing School Volunteer Roles

On another occasion when we met, Paul and Mary continued to discuss their perceptions of involvement and volunteer practices with the school. Although both parents visited Andrew's classroom, Paul was more involved at the school than Mary because she worked during school hours, but she visited the classroom occasionally. Their visits provided first hand information about school programs and the classroom's routine.

Mrs. Boston had no qualms about parents visiting or volunteering in her classroom. She also welcomed parents who wanted to participate as chaperones for class excursions. Paul served as a chaperone when the class visited the Science Museum. Mr. Keys stated,

> For some kids, it will be their first time going to the museum. They have a lot of exhibits there. This trip will give them a sense of where the earth is located in the solar system, and help them understand the planets. Andrew knows a lot about the museum. Of course, he has been there several times.

Classroom Routine: First Graders Learning to Write

During another conversation with Paul and Mary, they were asked about Mrs. Boston's classroom routine. Paul was well aware of what transpired in the classroom during the language arts block, because he was a participant. He described a writing activity.

> Every morning the class has to copy the morning news from the chalkboard. It is their penmanship assignment... It says, 'Today is Monday, April 27, 2005. It is sunny outside. It is the first day of the week. We are going to our science class.' The students get to practice writing and later they have an assignment where they make up a story. The teacher gives them a description of something like a car and they must write about it.

When he was asked about the specific classroom tasks he performed, Paul recounted,

> Mrs. Boston's assignments for me are to collect students' completed seatwork papers, place a sticker on them, or stamp a good job message on the papers, before placing them in a tray. I did not give the children grades, because that is the teacher's job.

Mary described what she observed one afternoon when she visited Andrew's classroom:

> When I visited the classroom in the afternoon, they were writing about a rain forest project that they had just completed. His class experimented and wrote about it for several days. Then they compiled a book. We're putting his booklet in a binder so that he will have something to reflect on, as he gets older.

PARENTAL INVOLVEMENT IN THE
LOCAL COMMUNITY AND BEYOND

Community involvement is one traditional context in which parents are involved in order to promote their children's learning. In-home and in-school participation are also included in this triage. Thus, parental involvement is centered around three contexts. In one of our conversations, Paul described how they were involved with their sons' education outside of local community and church settings.

For example, one year, they took the boys on vacation to visit Mr. Keys' hometown. Paul reported that they often took trips to keep their sons interested in learning new subject matter and to promote their learning.

This trip was significant, because they visited the university where Paul was enrolled as an undergraduate student.

> We also stress college. Last year, while on vacation, we took Andrew to visit my alma mater. His sister is a sophomore at that college. We believe that visiting college campuses now will have a positive influence on his attitude about higher education. That visit did actually boost his ego. As for teacher expectations, we have to reintroduce ourselves to the school staff every year and tell them what we expect from them.

Community Involvement and PTO Attendance versus Wednesday Night Bible Study

Despite the fact that parents' perceptions of the PTO varied greatly, we discussed what it meant to Paul and Mary. During our conversation, it was revealed that they were members of Pendleton School's PTO, but did not attend meetings. Instead, they participated in PTO programs. Mr. Keys explained,

> We are paid members of the Parent Teacher Organization. However, we don't attend PTO meetings because the meeting time conflicts with our work schedules and church activities. Otherwise, I would probably be more involved in that organization for two reasons. First, there is a lack of presence of African American parents on the PTO board. Second, few males participate in general.

The church was the vehicle for community involvement. Therefore, how this family perceived their involvement and practices with their child's education in the community was expressed in terms of their participation in church activities. As mentioned earlier in this chapter, Mary sang in the choir, Paul was a member of the deacon board; Joseph was in the youth choir and served on the youth usher board, while Andrew, the focal child, participated in the youth fellowship group. The family also attended Sunday school classes.

SUMMARY FOR CREATING POSITIVE INVOLVEMENT ROLES: EMBRACING ADVOCACY

Out of necessity, Mr. and Mrs. Keys became consumers in their child's education by choosing the schools he attended and networking in the neighborhood, to find the best teacher. School volunteering was their hallmark! This practice provided the family an up front and personal view of what was happening in the school. It was apparent that Paul and Mary were academically oriented, and stressed that their son strive for excellence, and uphold the moral values that built character. Moreover, their responses to interview questions addressed this couples' perceptions of their involvement and practices with the child's education in the home, the school, and in the community/church and beyond.

Parents As Advocates

Making the decision to send Andrew to speech therapy at an early age was an excellent idea. If Mary and Paul had waited until their son entered first-grade to initiate treatment for his speech impediment, perhaps he may not have made as much progress.
Early intervention was important because Andrew was able to work at his own pace, and on his own level, as he received one-on-one instruction. Fortunately, the speech and language strategies that Andrew learned enabled him to enter kindergarten on a level playing field with his peers (Blachman, 1998).

MY PERSONAL REFLECTIONS

These reflections make the connections between my past knowledge of parents as volunteers and advocates for their children relative to Mr. Key's experiences as a volunteer in his son's classroom and the parents' roles as advocates for their son.

Classroom Volunteers

Traditionally, mothers were involved in classrooms as volunteers and also assisted their children with literacy activities at home. Today, the script has flipped; fathers are assuming that role. Mrs. Boston was fortunate to have Mr. Keys as a volunteer in her classroom. When I was a classroom teacher, it never occurred to me to request a fathers' help. Had I asked, I wonder how many fathers would have volunteered? Mr. Keys conveyed that as a volunteer, he used the literacy activities that were taught at school to enhance Andrew's learning at home. The idea of father–child pairs in literacy activities was championed by Ortiz, Stile, & Brown (1999).

CHAPTER 4

RELIGION

The Umbrella for Parental Perceptions of Involvement

THE MAXWELL FAMILY

The Maxwell family consisted of David, the father; Ruth, the mother; Tammi, the focal child, who was 6 years of age; and Maryum, a toddler of 12 months. The couple had been married for 12 years. Both were born in Bellport and had attended Bellport Public Schools. Tammi was enrolled in a public school in the neighborhood. David and Ruth considered themselves first generation middle class.

The Maxwell's colonial house was located on a large, fenced-in, corner lot, with a large back yard and a half basketball court. On the first floor of the two-story home, there was a living room, formal dining room, kitchen, and den. In the living room, African art hung on the walls, and a bookshelf held children's books, toys, and the Bible. Family portraits and more books were on the built-in shelves on both sides of the fireplace.

Ruth had a Bachelor of Arts degree in communications from Brookford State University. Ruth had been employed as a club representative for a major Bellport transportation company, but she resigned from her position when her children were born. She explained, "I wanted to be at home with the children during their formative years."

David had an Associates of Arts degree in business administration from Bellport Community College and was employed as a firefighter. He was the

African American Middle-Income Parents, pages 29–36

first generation of his family to complete college. David informed me that his mother stressed the importance of a good work ethic.

This family attended church every Sunday and Bible study on Wednesday nights. Tammi was a member of the primary Sunday school class. Ruth sang in the choir, and David was a member of the men's fellowship group. The family lived by biblical principles and taught their children to obey the word of God.

When I talked with Reverend Elford, a scholarly, charismatic minister of a large church congregation in the Bellport community, he assured me that David and Ruth Maxwell would be an excellent couple with whom to interview. He described them as friendly, religious, open, honest, and cooperative.

First Meeting: Background Information

At the first meeting, the couple welcomed me into their home with open arms. We talked about family backgrounds. It was revealed that Ruth had grown up in a single-parent family and lived in section-eight housing; homes that are subsidized through federal funds and allocated to families who received public assistance. There were five children in Mrs. Maxwell's family and all of them completed college. Ruth was next to the youngest. She said, "I was the knee baby." (The knee baby is the toddler who sits on the mother's knee while an infant sibling is fed.)

Enthusiastically, Ruth made a point to stress her social background. She wanted me to know that she did not grow up in a middle class family. Ruth was not ashamed to admit that her family was considered low-income. Nonetheless, like her mother, she wanted the best education for her children. She shared that her mother was committed to education. She was instrumental in helping Ruth prepare for college and completed Ruth's applications and grant forms. Not surprisingly, Ruth was accepted to several colleges. Ruth also seemed delighted to report that she helped her mother study for the General Equivalency Diploma (GED). Ultimately her mom passed all of the examinations, and daughter and mother graduated from high school the same year.

Schooling Choices: Ensuring a Good Solid Based Education

In respect to choosing a school for Tammi, David and Ruth informed me of the reasons why they decided to send Tammi to a public school. Before it was time to register her for first-grade, they had a long discussion about which school setting would be best, a public or private educational institution. Tammi had attended a Catholic school for preschool and kindergarten and had progressed quite well. The parents were concerned about their child getting a good education: "We asked ourselves, can we send our child to a public school and feel comfortable that she is going to get the education that she needs?"

This was a huge decision for them and finally they decided to enroll Tammi in the neighborhood school. It was close to their home and one of the parents walked her to school and picked her up daily. In thinking about their dilemma and the major decision they had made, David and Ruth knew their involvement would be necessary. As David Maxwell stressed,

> We know what's out there, having gone through the educational system in the city of Bellport. We also understand that if we're going to be there to help her navigate through school, we will have to be there during the entire process, teaching her and helping her along the way. So, it is just as much for us as it is for her that we get involved, because we are concerned about her education.

PARENTS' EXPECTATIONS OF LITERACY DEVELOPMENT IN THE HOME

At this point in our discussions, I was interested in learning more about the educational expectations David and Ruth held for their first grader. I also hoped to gain some insight into how they viewed their perceptions and practices of literacy in the home. When asked what expectations they desired for Tammi, Ruth Maxwell was very specific about some short-term literacy goals:

> I think one of the biggest things that I want her to do is be able to pick up a book and be able to read and know what it means, not just read the words, but know what it means. I sit down and read with her but not as much as I'd like. Lately, it always seems like we're constantly running. However, I have started making adjustments... just about every night, during the past two weeks, one of us has read her a Bible story, because she has reminded us. I know she likes books. Obviously, if we don't sit down and take the time to read, then she's going to think it's not as important.

On the next visit to the Maxwell's house, we continued our conversation about reading. The parents were queried about the kind of books they read to their daughter. Mr. Maxwell stated while holding a Bible stories book,

> We read from this book. She enjoys these stories; there are questions at the end of each story and she can answer them. She also likes to read Dr. Seuss books and a variety of animal books.

Ruth also informed me about the type of home involvement practices in which they engage. She told me about a math activity she had chosen for Tammi to see if she understood the concept of money. She explained,

Last night, she told me that she was not sleepy. So, I said okay, go get your math book. We sat down and talked about the picture of two quarters in the book. It was the same ones she had problems with last night. I told her to go upstairs and get her barrette box and we counted the whole pile of barrettes together. We were up for a while last night! When I asked how many coins she saw in the book, she said, "Two." I then asked how much money it was and she kept saying two cents. We would count the barrettes again and she still said it was two cents instead of two quarters or fifty cents. It took us four hours to complete the math activity. I was glad that it was Friday and not a school night.

David added that,

Several weeks ago, we told you that we were teaching her how to count her lunch money; well she knows how to do that now.

In the area of homework, it was reported that completing first-grade homework was very new to this family, because Tammi was their first-born. As students themselves, over 30 years ago, Ruth and David did not remember having homework in first grade. Nevertheless, they worked hard to learn the first-grade homework routine. Ruth continued by describing her schedule:

Before we do any homework, I like to sit down and talk with Tammi about what went on in school that day and about doing her personal best in school. Every week, Tammi has a spelling test. The teacher sends home a list of words and tells the children to use each word in a sentence or write the words three times. Now that Tammi can read I have her sit down with the material that she needs and do her work. When she is done, I have her bring it back to me so that I can make sure it is neat and you can read what it says.

In ending this conversation, Ruth Maxwell held up a paper on which a yellow sticky was affixed. It had the directions for Tammi's weekly spelling assignment. They were clear and concise. She said, "This is what inspired us to become involved in Tammi's education!" According to Ruth, homework kept parents informed of the educational activities that transpired at school.

COMMUNICATION, PARENT–TEACHER
SATISFACTION, AND SCHOOL INVOLVEMENT

When the Maxwells needed to communicate with Mrs. Potter, Tammi's teacher, they no longer had to report to Mrs. Washington, the vice principal. Instead, they went directly to the first grade classroom. Mrs. Washington had been one of Ruth's elementary school teachers. This made school a more inviting setting and a place where communication was easy.

Therefore, Mrs. Maxwell comfortably focused on parent–teacher communication as it related to Tammi's school behavior. Ruth received a weekly progress report from the teacher stating that Tammi did not listen to directions during class time. Rather than visit the school to discuss the incident, she first discussed off task behavior with the child. "I want Tammi to respect Mrs. Potter." In response to the dilemma, however, Mrs. Maxwell shared how she communicated with her daughter relative to Mrs. Potter's comment on the progress report:

> The teacher sent us a note that said Tammi needed to work on her listening skill; so Tammi and I had a little talk. And after we had our talk, I had her sit down and write: "I will be a better listener" on two pages as a punishment. We sent the paper back to school with Tammi and directed her to apologize to Mrs. Potter for not listening. We wanted to make sure she understood that the teacher was the boss in the classroom. According to Ruth, in response to that problem, she also used a parable from the Bible to teach Tammi about obedience. (A parable is the brief storytelling method that appeals to the thinking and attitudes of listeners.)

The parent's religious beliefs guided how they dealt with their children, school curriculum, and school people. Once David and Ruth became concerned when the art teacher planned a Halloween lesson involving gargoyles. Because of their religious beliefs, they did not want their daughter to participate in the art lesson. Nor did they want her to be disrespectful to the art teacher. So, when Tammi told them what was going on in art class, the parents were concerned and took immediate action. As Mr. Maxwell stated,

> We don't celebrate Halloween, because we understand that the concept of Halloween is the celebration of evil. Also, we don't like gargoyles because of the statement they make. They are monsters! In the *Hunchback of Notre Dame,* the gargoyles got up and moved, and it was a hideous looking thing. We couldn't understand why the art teacher would give this activity to little kids. We told the vice principal about it, and then kept Tammi out of art class for a month. She worked with computers in the library rather than attend art class.

On another occasion, Mrs. and Mr. Maxwell objected to their daughter using dice and cards in her math class. In the future, before letting Tammi use these materials, the teacher asked the parents' permission. While David and Ruth were satisfied with the first grade teacher, it was revealed that they had negative feelings about the art teacher, because her art lesson interfered with their religious values. Ruth described how at ease they were with Mrs. Potter, Tammi's classroom teacher. She said,

> We are really comfortable with her teacher. I think it helps with parenting when you have a good teacher who understands and knows what parents expect of their children as far as getting a good education. That makes it easy for us. The teacher understands and knows what we expect. I think that as Tammi gets older, depending on the type of teacher she has, our involvement will increase.

Gender Balance Involvement: Dual Perceptions and Practices

Later in the year, David was asked about his perception of involvement with his daughter's schooling. How he saw himself with respect to Tammi's education is depicted in this story. He informed me that he walked his daughter to school and picked her up in the afternoon when his work schedule permitted. Moreover, when he walked Tammi to school, David also communicated with Tammi's teacher about her academic progress, if the teacher was available.

According to him, the highlight of his involvement was speaking to a group of excited, wide-eyed first graders about what he did as a firefighter. As David described it, "I volunteered to speak to Tammi's class about my challenging career." He described what happened when he entered the school dressed in his firefighter's uniform. David said,

> Dressed in my firefighter's uniform, I went to the school during Fire Prevention Week to speak with the kids about my profession. I explained what they could expect if there was a situation when the fire department had to come to their homes for a fire or a medical emergency. I also had the teacher dress up in one of the fire fighter's uniforms, mask, tank, the whole nine yards. The kids got a kick out of this presentation!

Mr. Maxwell volunteered to speak to his daughter's class about his career and the children learned priceless information about how to notify the fire department in case of an emergency. Building a partnership with teachers is important, because everyone involved can learn valuable information from parents by inviting them into classrooms as experts on a particular topic (Delpit 1988).

Developing Family Values: A Commitment to Education and Religion

David and Ruth had strong family values. Billingsley (1992) states that several family values revered by the African American family are strong commitments to education and religion. The Maxwell's espoused both of these values. As mentioned previously, they stressed a good education, because they wanted to prepare Tammi for the future. They were also actively involved in the church and taught their children biblical truths. For Ruth Maxwell, spending time with their daughter and teaching her basic skills were very important for her education. To ensure that Tammi would receive the best education possible, Ruth quit her job of ten years. She said she "wanted to spend quality time with her children and teach them." The family also gave up a once a year trip to a Caribbean Island. David Maxwell pointed out,

> We understand the sacrifices that need to be made for Tammi to get a good solid-based education. We just want Tammi to succeed. We bought her a computer with reading and math software. The computer program monitors her work, shows what she did well, and gives her a reward at the end. We want her to understand that if she studies now, she'll get a good job when she gets older.

As this conversation continued, the parents explained why they failed to participate in Parent Teacher Organization meetings. Their reasons were similar to the Keys family and most of the other parents that I interviewed, (i.e., PTO interferes with Bible study). Although, Mrs. Washington, vice principal of the school, had asked David and Ruth to participate, because the administrators needed more African American parents' involved in the PTO, they refused.

Mrs. Maxwell gave her perspective,

> We just can't attend PTO meetings, but we do attend functions such as assembly programs, carnival, field days, and potluck dinners. We can't lock ourselves into it, because we do other things with Tammi, as well as church activities on Wednesday nights.

David and Ruth Maxwell reported that their involvement in Tammi's education was not just for her but for her classmates as well. Comer and Haynes (1991) in their study with African American parents and their children noted that families' involvement within the school was important to children, because it improves the quality of education that all children received.

SUMMARY OF RELIGION: THE UMBRELLA
FOR PARENTAL INVOLVEMENT

However David and Ruth responded to questions about literacy learning, setting expectations, making choices, school satisfaction and crafting involvement roles, religion was the thread that connected their beliefs concerning parental involvement and practices. They saw Bible study as the compass needed to heed God's word during the week. David and Ruth embraced gender balance involvement and were participants in the three traditional contexts: the home, the school, and the community, through church activities. In relation to literacy development, it was their primary concern, because they wanted Tammi to receive a good education. For that reason, their home was immersed in the most popular children books, software, and instructional videos of popular television characters to enhance Tammi's literacy learning. They were not dollar poor. There is no doubt that they could afford the computer and school supplies to provide Tammi with a good education.

MY PERSONAL REFLECTIONS

Looking back at some of my school involvement practices, Mr. Maxwell's comments bring to mind the importance of volunteering in the classroom and building lasting educational partnerships with the teacher and the school in general.

Volunteering

One of my most memorable moments was serving as a volunteer in my son's kindergarten classroom. Among other activities, I enjoyed reading to children and chaperoning them on fieldtrips. I also remember how I made the entire kindergarten class wrist bracelets with bells on them as a holiday gift. The teacher and the students graciously thanked me for the gifts. My involvement demonstrated that my son's school and his classmates were important to me. In essence, I was there for my son and his friends.

CHAPTER 5

INVOLVEMENT ROLES

Not Fifty–Fifty

THE OWENS FAMILY

I first met the Owens family while attending services at Philemon Baptist Church with a friend. Donna and Charles Owens had relocated to Bellport from the Ohio area. Charles was a first-generation college graduate, who received his degree from Bellport University, where he was a star basketball player. At the time of this study, he was employed as an athletic director at the same university. Donna was a homemaker and a part-time student studying for a Bachelor of Arts Degree in elementary education. They had been married for 18 years and had two children. Charles Jr., six years of age, and Marsha, seventeen years of age. Both children attended public schools.

Mr. Owens reported that he came from a working middle-class family. After his grandparents retired, his parents became responsible for a restaurant business that had been in the family for over forty years. Charles and Donna considered themselves second-generation middle class, since Charles viewed his maternal grandparents as first-generation middle-class. The Owens' family were members of the Philemon Baptist Church. Donna was a leader of the youth group; Charles served on ad hoc committees upon request. Marsha and Charles Jr. attended the teen and primary Sunday school classes, respectively.

African American Middle-Income Parents, pages 37–45
Copyright © 2007 by Information Age Publishing

The First Meeting

The purpose of my first meeting was to learn about the family and Charles Jr., a first grade student. When I arrived, Marsha, the teenager answered the door and greeted me. After introducing herself, she announced my arrival, and left me to complete her science homework assignment. Donna then entered the room and offered me a seat and Charles followed. He greeted me in sweat suit and sneakers befitting his role as coach. Of course, a conversation about basketball ensued. Additionally, Charles informed me that he traveled frequently and our future meetings would have to be set around his schedule.

At this meeting, my main question for the parents was, "Tell me about your child and his school?" After I asked that question, there was silence in the room, as if one spouse was waiting for the other to speak. Finally, Donna spoke about Charles Jr.'s class placement. She remembered that when he was registered for first grade, they asked the administrator and first grade teachers to place him in a class with other African American males, because they lived in a neighborhood with very few African American children. Mrs. Owens explained:

> I selected Charles Jr.'s kindergarten teacher, but I did not know the first grade staff. Having volunteered in the kindergarten classroom throughout the school year, I knew most of the children in my son's class. When they promoted him to first grade, I knew that I didn't want him placed in the same class with certain children. So, I requested that they please separate my child from those children.

Mr. Owens added that they wanted their son to experience diversity. But, at the same time, they felt he needed at least one African American male child in his class, someone with whom he could identify. Charles Owens confessed: "We really wanted Charles Jr. to experience all types of children, but we did not want him to emulate bad behaviors."

PARENTAL INVOLVEMENT IN THE HOME

We Expect Him to be Responsible and Put Forth His Best Efforts

At the next meeting with the Owens, we discussed their expectations for Charles, Jr. in the first grade. Mrs. Owens was the first to give her perspectives on the topic. She reported that they had told Charles Jr. not to emulate any of the bad behaviors that his kindergarten classmates had portrayed. Donna continued to discuss their expectations for their son.

I expect him to get the best out of life, obey, and to do his best in school. I expect Charles Jr. to respect himself and his family, particularly his parents. I also expect him to trust others as much as he can and trust his own judgment. Most of all, I want him to be responsible and get a good education. So we spend time helping him with homework, especially spelling and writing. His 17-year-old sister also helps him with spelling.

In drawing on Donna Owens' statement about "expectations," I asked Mr. Owens what were his expectations of his son. He answered,

I expect Charles Jr. to be a good person in school. I also expect him to obey and not become a discipline problem. I think that discipline is very important. He is intelligent, and I just want him to put forth his best effort.

Father's Involvement Role: The Supporter

Charles Owens admitted spending less time with his son than his wife. He saw his role as "supporter," but he was also involved in his son's education when he was not working. Charles captured this sentiment particularly well:

I take Charles Jr. to school sometimes, stick my head in the door and speak to his teacher. If she is not busy, I might ask her about his progress. I also read to him and help with homework. Most of the time, it is my wife who checks to see how his day went, because, as I said, "I travel a lot!" But I do support everything she does!

Fathers' Nontraditional Role Definitions

Even though Charles Owens was less involved in his son's education and schooling than Donna, when at home, he did spend time reading to Charles Jr. and listening to him practice reading on his own. "Charles Jr. likes me to read to him at bedtime. I do that when I'm not traveling."

Mr. Owens also had concerns about the magnitude of his participation at his son's school. As an athletic director, he was not always in town and could not visit Charles Jr.'s classroom. Despite his unavailability, Charles Owens attempted to encourage his child's literacy learning and stressed the importance of physical fitness. He wanted Charles Jr. to go to school ready to learn and reach his academic potential. He explained,

Now that Charles Jr. is in first grade, we make sure he's prepared for school and arrives there on time. We see that he gets his rest at night, eats a good breakfast and that he's mentally ready to learn.

PARENTAL INVOLVEMENT IN THE SCHOOL

Awareness, Crafting Involvement Roles, and Promoting Learning

In a conversation with Donna and Charles concerning their son's daily classroom routine, I asked if they knew the first-grade schedule. Donna's response was, "I know that I am not the norm, and I also know that some parents work and cannot visit the school as much as I do." Not surprisingly, Donna stated that she spent more time at the school than the average first-grade African American parent. Consequently, her description of what transpired in the classroom sounded true. As I listened, it appeared as if she was visible at the school, with a camera, recording every activity. She confessed that when her son was in kindergarten, she had made it a point to volunteer every week or every other week. She quipped, "My own school load is heavy this year, and I can't visit as often." Now that her son was in first grade, she volunteered on Friday's, because it was a fun day for Charles Jr. and his classmates. Some Fridays, they took field trips or participated in other entertaining activities.

After driving him to school, Donna sometimes stayed around to help the teacher. By being visible, she was able to vividly describe what went on in her son's classroom. She began to describe a typical day by saying,

> First, they have the silent moment and the morning announcements. After that, they go into their separate reading groups. I believe it is called language arts. The teacher reads a story to the students after the language arts period. I know that they eat lunch at 11:00 AM. After lunch, they have math lessons. There are two math groups. Music or gym usually follows math, depending on the day of the week. At 2:50 PM, the children listen to the afternoon announcements, pack their book bags, get their coats, and wait for the bell to ring. When the bell sounds, it means that the busses are ready to load the children and take them home. A short time after, the bus numbers are called and the children depart as they hear their numbers.

This vivid description gave a clear picture of the teacher, Mrs. Shertzer's, first-grade activities and the classroom routine.

The School and Home Must Be in Agreement

Several weeks later, when I returned to the Owens' home, I learned how they promoted their child's learning. Mr. Owens easily told the story.

When I take Charles Jr. to school, I always take him to his classroom and talk with his teacher. It's also important that we keep a good relationship with his teacher, so that if there are any problems, we will know. I think we can encourage his learning by being involved... The home and school have to be in agreement. The more in agreement we are, the more we work together, and the more the child is going to learn. So working with the teacher is another way to encourage learning.

From Charles Owens' perspective, working with the school and being proactive were other ways to encourage learning. Moreover, he perceived that maintaining a good relationship with his son's teacher was also very important, because a child's home life and school performance are intricately related.

The Parental Role in Connection With the Child's School Activities

Other than volunteering in her son's classroom, there were other strategies that Donna used to promote Charles Jr.'s learning. She began telling me about these activities by giving me a chronology of her involvement with the school. Staring at the wall as if the activities were written in front of her, she mused,

We promote his learning by being involved in what he does at school. I forgot to tell you this before, but we went on a field trip to the apple and pumpkin farms in September. All trips are scheduled at the beginning of the school year. In December, we visited the museum for the lighting of the Christmas tree celebration. We also went to Constitution Theater to see Rudolph the Red-Nosed Reindeer. Winnie the Pooh was at that theater last month. I try to make all of the field trips! The children celebrated Black History Month in February. There was a classroom display of numerous books about African Americans. One Friday in February, children read poems by African Americans to their parents.

The Owens family attended many school activities such as, musical concerts, potluck meals, pasta nights, open houses, parent–teacher conferences, field trips and multicultural celebrations. Students in second through sixth grades performed in musicals under the supervision of the music teacher.

Donna and Charles enjoyed all of the school entertainment experiences immensely. Donna spoke excitedly about a particularly significant field trip.

One sunny day in the fall, the class walked one mile to visit the hospital's nursing program. They only stopped at the university long enough to eat lunch. The children learned how the nurses supported the doctors and other medical staff. They were also shown some of the medical equipment used to detect a disease and told how certain diseases were treated and cured.

According to Donna, this trip was a resounding success. The children were actively involved and learned a great deal.

Parents' Satisfaction With the Teacher and School: He Is at Grade Level

The Child's Progress Report

The March meeting with Donna and Charles revealed the results of their third parent–teacher conference. At that time, Mrs. Shertzer reported that Charles Jr. was reading at first grade level. When I asked the parents how their son learned to read, they informed me that Charles Jr. was read to from birth. The practice of reading to him continued during the preschool years, and remained throughout kindergarten and first grade. Therefore, it was easier for him to grasp the process when formal reading was introduced to the first graders. He closed with this comment,

> When parents are involved in the child's schooling, it makes the teachers' job easier. It also helps the child learn better. Children who are not read to in the home tend to have a hard time learning to read. If they have a rough home life, it is hard for them to learn at school. So it is important for the school and the home to work together.

Mr. Owens continued,

> Charles Jr. is reading at grade level, because we laid the foundation before he went to kindergarten. What I mean is, we exposed him to different activities such as visits to the zoo, museums, teaching him letters, sounds, and shapes. My wife did a good job; now she monitors what he is doing at school.

Schooling Satisfaction: The Teacher and Administrator

On another occasion when I met with Donna and Charles, I asked if they were satisfied with the teacher and administrator. Charles responded,

> I am not quite as involved in the day-to-day activities as my wife. Our son entered Green School for kindergarten, and now, after having been there for eight months as a first grader, I can truthfully say, it is going well and Charles Jr. admires his teacher.

According to Mr. Owens, the school environment was a safe haven for his son. As a result, Charles Jr. was able to get his schoolwork accomplished without distraction. "Yes," Mrs. Owens agreed, "I am happy with the school. I think they do a good job!"

Furthermore, Charles and Marsha Owens expressed their satisfaction with Mrs. Shertzer. They thought she was a hands-on type teacher and spent individual time with the kids. "I don't really know her that well, but our child seems to be happy and is enjoying first grade," declared Charles.

Moreover, Donna Owens balanced this conversation by adding more personal information about the teacher. She stated,

> I like Mrs. Shertzer. She pushes them to read! I think first graders need that petting and nurturing, and I think she gives that also. The rumor around the school is that she's the best teacher as far as challenging children to accelerate in reading. I didn't have any input in which first-grade teacher he would get, but I have found that challenging kids to read is Mrs. Shertzer's niche.

PTO Meetings: Too Many Other Activities

After discussing teacher and school satisfaction, we explored their perspectives on the parent–teacher organization (PTO). I asked them if they had been involved with the PTO during the school year. The answer was no, but they had attended several evening PTO functions. Mrs. Owens expressed her reasons.

> I am not involved in the school's PTO this year, because I have a class on Wednesday nights. I was going to Bible study on Wednesday nights, but now I can't attend those classes either. My evenings are pretty full with my children's extracurricular activities. I really don't want to slight Charles Jr., but I just haven't taken the time to get involved with the PTO this year.

PARENTAL INVOLVEMENT
IN THE CHURCH AS THE COMMUNITY

From a biblical perspective, the local church taught the moral values to which this family adhered. According to Donna, "We expect our children to participate in church activities, and set a good example for them to follow." She also said that she was the leader of the youth group, Charles served on ad-hoc committees when available, and the children were members of the youth ministry. Marsha was a member of the basketball team at her school and she participated in a recreational program at the church. Charles Jr. was a member of the pee wee basketball team at the church. According to Donna, she and Charles led by example, and the children followed, because it was the Godly thing to do. Charles said, "I am teaching my daughter to coach basketball, because, one day, she might have the opportunity to manage her own team."

SUMMARY FOR INVOLVEMENT ROLES: NOT FIFTY–FIFTY

Mr. and Mrs. Owens advocated for Charles Jr.'s placement in a setting that allowed him to be with other African American boys. They wanted him to follow school protocol. Therefore, high expectations, good behavior, and life skills such as obedience, trust, caring, and responsibility were stressed. According to Dorothy Rich (1988), life/mega skills are the core values, the attitudes, and the behaviors that determine success in school and on the job. The parents were contented with the progress Charles Jr. made in reading. They were also satisfied with the teacher and school in general. Because of his job, Mr. Owens was unavailable to participate at the school. However, he did participate in his son's literacy development in the home, and Donna volunteered in the classroom and participated in other school and home activities. Though not fifty–fifty in terms of time commitments, both parents were strong examples of positive family involvement.

Fathers As Supporters

Some parents have used the term *supporter* to describe an involvement role (Eccles & Harold, 1993; J. L. McAdoo, 1997). Mr. Owens used the word supporter because he was less involved with his son's education than his spouse. Hence, he viewed himself as the supporter. While ongoing involvement was challenging, Charles Owens said he supported what his wife did with their son. He meant that he supported all learning activities that Donna taught Charles Jr., and he also provided emotional and financial support as well.

MY PERSONAL REFLECTIONS

As I recall, during my days as administrator, parent, and teacher, few African American parents were involved in parent–teacher organizations (PTO). Lack of involvement in this domain precluded them the opportunity to network in the school setting.

In comparing the Owens family to other families in this book, involvement was not always equal. I am reminded of my own life and can relate to this family because my spouse was not always involved with schooling activities. However, like Mr. Owens he was caring and genuinely supported what I did to help our son succeed in school.

PTO Involvement

When my son was in first grade, I tried to attend parent–teacher organization meetings. I made the majority of them despite being enrolled in administration and supervision classes. It was not easy to make the meetings after having worked all day, but my involvement was necessary because I cared about the school and was interested in my child's education. As a PTO member at the high school, I held the office of secretary and served as fund-raising chairperson at the middle school. To inspire more parents to attend PTO meetings, the class with the most parents present at a meeting were given a pizza party. If my memory is correct, Mitchell's class won the party once.

CHAPTER 6

INVOLVEMENT AND SOCIALIZATION PRACTICES FOR SELF-SUFFICIENCY

THE PENNEY FAMILY

The Penney family lived in a large split-level ranch house in a small community very close to Bellport. In this neat and well-furnished home, the lower level playroom was filled with toys, books, and other materials, including a computer and reading and math software used to complete school-related tasks. Kathy and Thomas had been married for 14 years, and had two children, 2-year-old Justin, and Justine, the focal child. Justine was enrolled in a Seventh-Day Adventist School. I became acquainted with Kathy Penney through one of my college sorority sisters. When I explained my research concerning parent involvement in early literacy development, she and Thomas agreed to be interviewed.

Thomas Penney was born in the midwest. He was first in his family to complete his secondary education at a boarding academy and the first to graduate from college. He held a Bachelor of Arts degree in theology and a Master of Arts divinity degree. Reverend Penney was the pastor of the Seventh-Day Adventist Church in Bellport, and sat on the board of directors for the related private school attended by his daughter, Justine. Kathy Penney, a native New Yorker with roots in the West Indies, had a Bachelor of Arts degree in business administration and accounting. She was currently enrolled in a masters online program and employed as a business teacher in the higher education department at Mansville College.

African American Middle-Income Parents, pages 47–55
Copyright © 2007 by Information Age Publishing

While Kathy and Thomas were from working-class families, they considered themselves first-generation middle class. They were also first-generation college graduates. Kathy confessed that her parents instilled the idea of getting a good education. Kathy and Thomas stressed the same with their daughter, Justine.

The First Meeting

At the first meeting Kathy and Reverend Thomas Penney seemed to understand how parental involvement promoted children's success in school. It was, however, Kathy who was more verbal regarding the topic; Thomas let Kathy take the lead. However, he began contributing more frequently when he became comfortable with the educational jargon.

Choices for Religious Reasons

Reverend Thomas Penney's role as church pastor allowed for a lot of family religious practice. Every Sabbath, they attended church and church school. Pastor Penney, also worked with the youth group. So, for Kathy and Thomas Penney, school choices were made for religious reasons. They sent their daughter to the Seventh-Day Adventist School in the Bellport area. When I asked them about their decision, Mrs. Penney responded,

> The philosophy that is taught at the Adventist School is more in line with what we believe about religion; I like the idea that they have prayer. We don't have to worry about how evolution is presented. They present creation from a biblical perspective.

Furthermore, Mrs. Penney was pleased with the class size, the teachers, and the administration. She stated,

> The classes are small, and there is more one-on-one contact between the students and teachers. A small class size influences the teacher's ability to provide individualized instruction to the multiage group.

Mrs. Penney revealed that Mr. Poole, Justine's teacher, taught a small combination class consisting of first through third grade students. Being a first year teacher who had just graduated from college, Kathy perceived that he was doing a good job.

Fostering Parental Involvement Through Communication and Receptivity

Once, when I visited the family, I asked them additional questions about Justine's school. Kathy's response was, "I like the fact that the teachers and administration are very receptive to new ideas." She proceeded to elaborate on her comment.

> At the beginning of the school year, the principal sent home a survey asking every parent which programs they would like to have implemented at the school. I suggested that they have a spelling bee. As a result of my recommendation, the school had grade-level spelling bees this year. I don't know if I was the only one who made the suggestion, but I am glad that I spoke up, because my daughter won first place in the first-grade spelling contest. She also won first place in the science fair.

Kathy expressed how surprised she was that her input was considered. She later admitted that she submitted the idea because she wanted Justine challenged in spelling, an important area of literacy learning.

When Justine told her parents that she also wanted to enter a butterfly project in the education fair, the parents were elated to learn about her interest in science and they supported her efforts. The spelling bee was scheduled to take place during the month of May at the education fair. Kathy had requested a day off from work so that she was available to attend the education fair along with Thomas and their son, Justin. According to Thomas Penney, attending the education fair was a highlight for the family because of Justine's success. She was one of the youngest children in her class, and the champion, because she won first place in the spelling bee and the science fair.

Kathy strikes at the heart of the matter when she described helping Justine with the science project.

> I gave her some guidance for the science project but she used her computer skills to research butterflies. While she was planning her presentation for the exhibit on butterflies, I told her to do her best.

Kathy is a technology teacher. According to her, she taught Justine how to operate the computer before the child entered first grade. Justine had the latest software, instructional videos, and computer games to enhance learning. She wanted to plan the science project without her mother's assistance. Mrs. Penney, however, believed that as the parent it was her role to guide her daughter through the process and provide her with materials.

PARENTAL INVOLVEMENT IN SCHOOL

Constructing Manageable Involvement Roles

Being a minister, Reverend Penney's working hours began when Mrs. Penney's workday ended. He wanted to be more involved at Justine's school, but he cared for their 2-year-old son while his wife worked. Before the birth of his son, he had Monday morning devotions at Justine's school. Nevertheless, he did read to his daughter, and assisted with the spelling bee and homework assignments. Thomas said, "To prepare Justine for the spelling bee, I had been going over the old spelling words and making sure that she was comfortable and ready as can be!"

Thomas and Kathy attended parent conferences and school-wide holiday activities. At the winter parent–teacher conference they spoke with Mr. Poole and asserted their ideas about Justine's academic progress. Kathy expressed her concerns about Justine's literacy development and her fear that Justine might become bored with learning.

> Justine is opinionated, strong willed, and very smart. However, she is a little shy and needs to be challenged, especially in reading. I am concerned about her reading skills. She could benefit from extra help in that area of learning. She must be pushed or she'll get bored. She also has mastered the math and should move to the next levels.

Additionally, Thomas and Kathy enjoyed attending the holiday celebration at the school.

> We attended a musical comedy and Justine had a small part in the play. It was about Joseph and Mary on their way to Bethlehem. The children seemed to enjoy it. We were pleased; it was a joy to see her perform. The play was basically for all grades.

Father's Involvement in Local, Regional, and Educational Seventh-Day Adventist Matters

Reverend Thomas Penney was the pastor of a Seventh-Day Adventist Church, and served as executive secretary for the governing board of all Seventh-Day Adventist Churches in the eastern geographical region. In addition, he sat on the board of directors for the private school his daughter attended in the Bellport area. There were between 10 and 15 members on the board and they set policy for all financial matters including tuition payment, application review, granting admission and disciplinary problems. Mrs. Penney stated that she once served as treasurer of the board. As a member of the board, Thomas discussed the policy they used to select new uniforms for students. Reverend Penney described his participation as follows:

> Every month we meet to discuss the school's needs, and any outstanding committee reports are given at that time. In May, the uniform committee submitted its proposal to the board. They suggested price changes and different uniform colors. They hadn't discussed shoes, but we said students wouldn't be able to wear sneakers except for gym. They would have to wear their black or blue shoes to match the uniform. After discussing the shoes, the proposal was approved.

Mrs. Penney revealed that her husband had been instrumental in helping to make a grading policy change while serving on the board.

> At the beginning of the school year, when the board met to discuss giving actual grades to first graders, Thomas was asked his opinion because our daughter was entering first grade. In the past they were giving children S's and U's to indicate progress, but now traditional letter grades (e.g., A, B, and C) appeared on report cards and also on the honor roll.

Thomas said when they asked his opinion about the grade change he thought it was a good idea to use alphabetical grades, because children could equate the meanings to failing or making progress. The letter grades also showed them the fruits of their labor, especially when their names appeared in the quarterly newsletter.

PARENTAL INVOLVEMENT IN THE HOME

After discussing the parents' involvement with school activities, our conversations turned to involvement in the home relative to schooling and education. When asked what was done to enhance the child's learning in the home. Mr. Penney responded,

> What we are doing now is creating a comfortable homework environment. We are making sure she has the proper materials with which to work. She has pens, pencils, paper, crayons, and glue. I mean she has access to just about anything she may need to complete an assignment. Of course, she has use of the computer.

Mrs. Penney revealed that they were also helping Justine find the answers to questions by using the computer. According to Kathy, they expected her to know how to use the computer and its software for reading, math, science, and other subjects.

Justine wanted to know what caused facial moles and where they come from. So, I told her we're going to get on the computer, go to the *Kids Site,* and find the answers to her questions. Then I taught her how to search for other questions without supervision from us.

Expectations: For the Teacher, the Child, and the Parent

Expectations for the Teacher and Parent

Later in the year, Kathy, Thomas, and I discussed their perceptions of involvement and practices with regard to expectations. When I asked about teacher expectations, Reverend Penney was the first to respond. Being a member of the board at his daughter's school, he talked generally about his expectations of teachers and parents in terms of accountability. Thomas believed that parents and teachers should be held accountable for children's education. He perceived that they should be committed to the same goal, (i.e., a good education). He could not or did not want to separate these two roles. In other words, parent and teacher roles seemed to be woven together, creating a seamless connection. He affirmed,

> You have to let the teacher know that your child's education is important to you, and that you're going to hold her accountable to do her part in the educational process, and in turn, teachers should hold us accountable. If children see that we are involved, then they are more interested and feel a sense of emotional support. If they know that it is a unified body dealing with them, it adds to their comfort level.

For Reverend Penney, a unified body entailed cooperation between parents and teachers, thus building a positive rapport. Furthermore, he continued,

> You know, the teacher must feel comfortable enough to come to us if there is a concern. They must not feel like, "oh no, this child is having a problem. Oh, my goodness, now I have to deal with that parent." We should never put the teacher in the position of avoiding us. It's just going to affect our child negatively.

Expectations for the Child

To continue our dialogue about expectations relative to parental involvement roles, I asked Thomas and Kathy, "What are your expectations of your daughter?" Kathy responded by first telling me about how she perceived her role as a parent. She explained,

> First and foremost, I love my child and want to do everything I can to give her the benefits of a good education. Second, it is my responsibility. I brought this child into the world. So I have to do everything in my power to make sure that all of her needs are met and that she is not devoid of anything, because we failed to carry out our responsibility.

Reverend Penney added to the conversation,

> We expect her to do well in school and to ask the teacher questions when she does not understand a word or how to work a math problem. Mr. Poole will take the time to help her, because he gives one-on-one attention to his students. He is very capable; that is why the board hired him.

Mrs. Penney fervently continued to explain,

> Justine must be able to compete. We have made sure that whatever is the latest technology she will be able to access it. Now my daughter is able to go to the computer, put in her CD, and do her work. So we expect her to do this, and we're trying our best to ensure that she has access to the latest tools. Even here at home, we encourage her to read to both of us. We stress daily reading.

Creating a Home Literacy Environment

Several weeks later, I met with Thomas and Kathy. I began our conversation by asking how Justine was progressing with reading. Kathy Penney responded,

> Justine is a smart child, but when she left kindergarten, she was least prepared in reading. I recently had her tested, because I was concerned. I'm not satisfied with that result, so I plan to do some work with her in reading this summer. My goal is to improve her reading, that's our focus right now. We were just talking about that yesterday. As a matter of fact, this summer, we are going to really work on it with her! We have also thought about home schooling as an option.

In planning for the summer, Kathy revealed that helping her daughter with reading would have a positive effect on Justine's literacy development. She also believed they already modeled for Justine the importance of reading. Kathy said,

> She sees us reading the Bible, books, newspapers, magazines, or writing church sermons. She also sees me studying for my masters degree. I believe she knows that education is important to us. Justine already has a library card. When she goes to the library, I plan to steer her to the literacy section that's appropriate for her age and let her pick out the books she likes to read.

Interestingly, when Mrs. Penney had her daughter tested, the results revealed that Justine was a half year behind in reading at midyear. By teaming closely with Mr. Poole, the first-grade teacher, and working with her daughter during the summer, Kathy anticipated significant gains in Justine's reading.

A Good Education for Independency and Self-Sufficiency

In my privileged position as the researcher, I listened to Kathy and Reverend Penney as they spoke of their daughter's ability to become literate in terms of future desires and present day-to-day aspirations. I asked, "What does it mean for Justine to obtain a good education?" Mrs. Penney revealed this moving account:

> Justine has to be able to support herself. She has to obtain enough knowledge, to ensure that she will be hired and not have to be dependent on anyone to necessarily provide a living for her. That means she has to be self sufficient, and the only way to do that is to finish school, not just high school, but to go to college as well.

According to Kathy, they wanted their daughter to receive a good education, complete school, get a good professional position, and make enough money to take care of herself and live the American dream.

BEYOND PTA: FAMILY INVOLVEMENT IN THE COMMUNITY

The parents were later asked about their involvement in the parent–teacher association (PTA). Mrs. Penney conveyed that she was unable to participate, because the school did not have an organized PTA. Instead, the administration asked retired church members to assist with those activities that normally would have been implemented by the parent–teacher association (PTA). When the school had fund-raisers it was the secretary and retirees who planned these events and collected the money for them. Mrs. Penney said,

> Justine and I went up and down the streets in our community selling Dine-a-Mate books to the neighbors. We sold 10 books at $25.00 each and made a total of $250.00 for the school. The school has three big fund-raisers per year and bake sales throughout the year. This year they had fruit, Dine-a-Mate books, and a book fair. I always buy a box of fruit from Florida and I volunteer to assist with the evening book fair.

Reverend Penney explained,

> We think education is a three-prong process: church, school, and home; all three are constantly working together to educate the child. For example, the year-end excursion to Sea Breeze Amusement Park is a family affair. The school requests that all families attend and chaperone their children. We travel on the bus with other families. Everyone helps to supervise their own children and others as well. It is a fun day for all!

SUMMARY OF SOCIALIZATION PRACTICES FOR SELF-SUFFICIENCY

The Penney family chose the private school setting because the school's philosophy was more in line with their own. They set high expectations for Justine according to their beliefs. Reverend Penney was an advocate of holding parents and teachers accountable for children's education. He perceived that a partnership between the home and the school would provide children with a good education. Knowing the importance of literacy learning, Mrs. Penney envisioned a massive intervention plan to assist Justine with reading skills. They knew that reading was a key ingredient in improving Justine's technology skills. Therefore, empowering Justine with quality literacy skills was their goal; they wanted her prepared for the information age work force.

MY PERSONAL REFLECTIONS

Thinking about my involvement roles as a parent many years ago, helps me relate to how Thomas and Kathy expressed their expectations for their daughter, Justine, and her teacher, Mr. Poole. I can see a great deal of value in the way this family reported their expectations. Their ideas served as a road map for what their daughter and her teacher needed to do and a blueprint of the parent's feelings.

Setting Expectations

When our son, Mitchell, was a toddler and later a preschooler, we knew what our academic expectations were for him. That is, we wanted him to continue the progress that he had made in reading and math and other subjects. We articulated this to his teacher(s) each year. Taking little for granted, we sat him down and slowly explained what we expected of him at the Montessori school, at home, and at church. Most of his teachers followed through with our expectations.

CHAPTER 7

PERCEPTIONS OF INVOLVEMENT AND MICROMANAGING A CHILD'S EDUCATION

THE PHILLIS FAMILY

I met Ester at a sorority function ten years ago. At the time she was single. Later she met and married Reverend Joshua Phillis. They lived on the upper west side of Bellport. Joshua and Ester have four daughters. Connie, the focal child, and her siblings attended Catholic schools. Their colonial brick house had five bedrooms, and two and a half baths on the top level. A living room and formal dining room, a large kitchen, a half bath, and a sitting area were located on the first floor. Their sitting/study area had a fireplace, television, a musical keyboard, a chalkboard, computer, printer, software, books, and other educational materials.

Ester graduated from Bloomfield University with a Bachelor of Arts degree in Biology and held a Masters degree in chemistry from Whitnum University. She worked as a biologist for several years, and became a homemaker after leaving that position due to an illness. Reverend Phillis had a Bachelor of Arts degree in chemistry and was a teacher in the Bellport School System. Coming from working-class families, their parents had high school educations and were employed as factory workers. Both Joshua and Ester were the first in their families to graduate from college; they considered themselves first-generation, middle class. Reverend Phillis was from

African American Middle-Income Parents, pages 57–64
Copyright © 2007 by Information Age Publishing

North Carolina and Mrs. Phillis was born in Brooklyn, New York. The family attended church every Sunday. All of their children sang in the choirs at their respective schools and in the church choir. The girls also had a gospel quartet. They went to various churches ministering for the Lord in song. While they did not charge a fee for their services, oftentimes, the church leadership gave them a donation. According to the parents, the girls deposited their money in a savings account.

I remembered that Ester's youngest daughter had entered first grade in the fall, so I called her to inquire of her interest and availability to participate in my parent involvement study. With enthusiasm, she said they would be happy to participate. I mailed her a consent form. When it was returned, I called them and we set dates and times for several interviews.

MAKING CHOICES TO ENHANCE
ACADEMIC ACHIEVEMENT

The First Meeting

During our first interview, Joshua and Ester began immediately talking about their decision for sending their daughters to Catholic schools. When Reverend and Mrs. Phillis' oldest daughter, Esterlean, was in first grade, she was not learning to read and this concerned them greatly. Similar to Schmidt's (1998) study, they sensed cultural conflict among the students and between the teacher and themselves. During their first visit to the classroom, they experienced negative cultural chaos. They reported that the children were fighting, making racial remarks toward one another, and had little respect for the teacher, and she seemed not to care. The teacher also failed to entertain any of the parent's suggestions. The Phillis' withdrew their daughter from that school immediately. According to them, they had her tutored, but this support did not improve the child's reading skills. Mrs. Phillis further explained,

> Even though our oldest daughter, Esterlean, was getting the stimulation at home, she was falling through the cracks, because she wasn't being taught to read at school. Out of frustration and fighting with the teacher, school administrators, and finally the school board, we transferred her to St. Andrew's for a better education, discipline, and structure. It was not the same there. The classes were smaller. If her grades did not improve, we could raise hell, because we were paying for her education.

At St. Andrew's, Esterlean gradually began to read. At the time that I was visiting Joshua and Ester, she was enrolled in Dominican, a Catholic middle school, and was on the honor roll. Ester said it was as if a light bulb went on in Esterlean's head and she saw the big picture. Therefore, they decided to enroll the other children, in St. Andrew's when they were ready for first grade. Connie, the focal child was the last to enroll at the school. Her sister was a third grader there.

PARENTAL INVOLVEMENT IN THE HOME

Children Learning to Learn Through Study Skills

During one of my visits, all of the girls, including the first grader, were studying for tests by learning to recall previous information that had been taught at school. They would need to apply this knowledge at a later date. According to Mrs. Phillis, "her daughters did not wait until the night before to study for tests." Instead, she promoted their learning by motivating them to study regularly and practice what they had learned. To help them improve their memory, they used organization strategies for recall and acronyms, acrostics, and other association techniques. When they had completed their assignments, they read for recreation.

Jumping Through Hoops: Seeking the Best Education for My Girls

To ensure that their girls received a good education, Ester and Joshua emphasized good study habits. To illustrate, Mrs. Phillis said,

> It's our duty to see that our children get the best education possible. If that means jumping through hoops, I will jump through them to do it. It's also our duty to instill in them good study habits.

Mrs. Phillis did not mince words when it came to her children's education. She used the metaphor "jump through hoops" to emphasize just how important it was for her children to receive a good education. According to Joshua, Mrs. Phillis was the boss, because she seemed to micro-manage everything that dealt with their children's education. At one of my visits with the family, Joshua described Ester as the "enforcer" because of how she perceived her involvement and reported practices with the children's education. In terms of watching or overseeing, he also said she reminded him of a part of Proverbs 31:27, which states: "A virtuous woman carefully watches all that goes on in her household..." In his mind's eye, Ester Phillis personified that virtuous woman.

A Father's Perception of Literacy Learning in the Home

As I continued to interview the family, they got to know and trust me. Thus, I felt comfortable asking Joshua and Ester almost any question about their perceived involvement and the roles they crafted for themselves. On an evening that winter, when I arrived for an interview, Joshua Phillis was reading to Connie. I asked, "Who helps Connie with homework?" This was a question that had been bothering me for several months. I wanted to know if Joshua was always involved with Connie's education, and if so, how was he involved. Reverend Phillis was the first one to respond to my question about homework. He said, "I'm engaged with my daughters' schooling and believe in at-home involvement."

When Connie wanted to read, Mr. Phillis taught her to read from the Bible. They wanted her to enter first grade reading. Consequently, Joshua Phillis acknowledged that one of their responsibilities was to nurture and guide Connie through the early reading process. Reverend Phillis explained,

> Bible stories inspired our first grader to read. At about age 4, I would read to her at night. We have this one little children's Bible that has a lot of pictures in it; I read it to her and eventually, she would read to me. Basically, she was looking at pictures. On Sundays, she would take her Bible to church, and when they said turn to a particular scripture, she would turn to the pages. Then she started reading. She really wanted to do what the others were doing.

Homework: The Bridge Connecting the Home and the School

The Phillis' believed that Connie was successful in school, because they were involved with her homework and volunteered in the school. The parents viewed homework as the lens through which the home and school were united as a seamless link. In other words, home activities were a continuation of the schools' work. Joshua Phillis explained, "the children know what is expected of them when they come home from school, the first thing they have to do before they play is get their homework competed."

Ester Phillis supported her husband's response by saying,

> If they don't have homework, I give them some. After the homework is done, they have to bring it to me so that I can check it. If it is not right, we keep working. They cannot pass and neither can they understand what was taught during the day if they don't spend some time practicing in the afternoon. To keep them academically focused, they are not allowed to watch television during the week!

As revealed by the parents, assisting with homework provided a vehicle for them to link the home and the school together as a continuous chain. Moreover Ester stated that homework increased the child's chances for learning good study habits, by practicing in the home those skills learned at school.

PARENTAL INVOLVEMENT IN THE SCHOOL

Role Construction, School Awareness, Communication, and Satisfaction

A Kaleidoscope Vision of the First Grade Schedule

One afternoon I met with Joshua and Ester. We discussed ways in which they crafted involvement roles, knowledge of the school's routine, communicating with school people, and schooling satisfaction. As I thought back to how Joshua had explained his involvement with Connie's literacy learning, I realized that Joshua was indeed involved with Connie's schooling at home and in the church. In light of his involvement, I queried Ester Phillis about how she defined her involvement roles. Ester perceived that her involvement with Connie's education and schooling was through Joshua. One of the roles she had constructed for herself was to volunteer in the school on a regular basis. When asked if she was aware of the school's routine, she described how it differed from what transpired in public schools. Ester explained,

> They start school at 7:45 AM, and at 8:00 AM, they have prayer. Then they go into the regular schoolwork, such as reading, math, and spelling. Connie does well in all of these subjects. At 11:00 AM, they have lunch. I know that they pray at lunchtime. Other than that, the day is like the routine in a public school. For instance, they have gym, art, and music twice a week. Social studies and science are usually taught in the afternoon.

From this description, Ester presented a kaleidoscopic vision of what the school day resembled. According to her, she was visible in the school, because she volunteered three days a week in the cafeteria or in the classroom if needed.

Teacher Expectations and Communication

Mrs. Phillis frequently communicated with Connie's teacher about the child's academic progress. She said, "Parents' involvement in schools is beneficial, and children are treated better when such involvement occurs." Since she was at the school weekly, Ester expected the teachers to inform her of any problems her two daughters encountered in a timely manner. She emphasized,

> I let teachers know that if there is anything going on with my children, I want to know right away about any kind of problem, whether it's with academics or with their behavior. I don't want to find out about a problem later.

According to Mrs. Phillis, Connie's teacher, Sister Catherine, was responsive to her request. She viewed Connie as a model student, behaviorally and academically. Connie was on the honor roll and had been promoted to second grade at midyear. Thus far, she had perfect attendance.

In Ester's opinion, she wanted to keep the doors of communication open so that everyone, including the child, would be on the same page. With regard to communicating with teachers about cumulative grade, this matter was discussed at parent–teacher conferences.

> I attend parent–teacher conferences to keep informed of overall grade point averages for each child. Of course, I attend four times as many conferences as the average parent who has one child, because I have two girls at St. Andrew's catholic, another at Our Lady of Hope, and one at Dominican, a Catholic middle school. I also attend open houses at these schools.

When asked about her involvement with the Parent Teacher Association (PTA), Mrs. Phillis replied,

> At St. Andrew's school, they know that I do not attend PTO meetings, because I volunteer three days. If I tried to go to all of my children's schools, then I would have to attend three PTO meetings and that would take its toll on me. However, I do participate in the others girls' schools when they have programs and I bake for fund-raisers. Sometimes I serve as a chaperone on field trips for all of my girls. I did that when I was working. I would just take the day off from work and help with transportation, because the Catholic Schools do not provide bussing for excursions.

Satisfaction With Schooling: A Mother's Opinion

Later, during the year, I arrived at the Phillis' home and was greeted by Connie. She informed her parents that I had arrived, and then she disappeared in the den with a book. Both parents greeted me and invited me to sit at the table. I was interested in exploring the parent's perceptions of the school environment and the school people. At the beginning of our conversation, I asked if they were satisfied with Connie's teacher, and Sister Martha, the principal of the school. Without hesitation Mrs. Phillis replied,

I am very satisfied with the school overall. I like the teachers and the principal. I think we really work well together, but sometimes I think the principal could be a little firmer with students and teachers. My only concern is that she tries to please everybody and, in her quest to please everybody, sometimes ends up pleasing nobody. On a scale of one to ten, I would give her a three.

According to Ester, she experienced contentment knowing that their children would attend a school with teachers that she was pleased with and trusted. Despite her rating of the principal, she indicated that they had a workable relationship.

FAMILY INVOLVEMENT IN THE COMMUNITY

Family and Church: Ministry Through Song

The Phillis family was involved in the community through church participation. As revealed earlier, the girls organized a gospel quartet and advertised their program and availability to minister for the Lord in song at various churches. The oldest girl explained,

As part of children's ministry, we organized this singing group, because we wanted other people to hear us sing and praise the Lord, instead of singing hip hop songs. Sometimes we are asked to sing at churches in the local community and at some that are as far as three hours away from the city of Bellport.

SUMMARY OF INVOLVEMENT
AND MICROMANAGEMENT

Dissatisfied with the public school, the Phillis family sent their daughter, Connie, to St. Andrew's, a Catholic school, to receive a better education. By crafting an involvement role in the area of literacy learning, Reverend Phillis taught Connie to read before she entered first grade. Similar to the fathers in Lamb's (1997) study, Joshua was nurturing in the role as caregiver and teacher of literacy, and this appeared to be good for Connie's literacy development. Ester volunteered at St. Andrew's school three days per week. She communicated their desires and aspirations for Connie to her teacher and the principal. As a result of frequently volunteering in the school, Ester knew St. Andrew's curriculum and daily classroom routines. Although she was satisfied with the school and admired Connie's teacher, she had some concerns about Sister Martha, the principal.

MY PERSONAL REFLECTIONS

The mirror in my mind recalled a past parental involvement experience that occurred over two decades ago relative to our expectations for my son's school. I can connect to Ester Phillis stated involvement and practices with their child's teacher as she requested that they notify her of any major behavior or academic problems in a timely manner so that the episode(s) could be resolved.

Parental Expectations for Teachers

When my son, Mitchell, was in elementary school, I remember communicating the same information to his teachers. I will share an incident that happened to me during his senior year. It was the kind of phone call you would never forget. "Your son did not show up for class today," a voice whispered on the other end of the line. "We know your expectations but we do not expect you to leave your office now, but we thought you should know." I immediately informed my secretary that I had to leave as soon as possible. I did not know where to look for my son, but I headed to the high school to get more information. When I arrived in the office, I saw other parents whose children were graduating seniors and I knew right away that my son, and other seniors, had taken the day off to celebrate their upcoming graduation. The principal ushered us into his office and told his story. The counselors knew where the students were and everything was under control. They were safely celebrating at the park and beach area about 5 miles away from the school. I thanked the principal for calling me and returned to my office. The teachers, counselors, and administrators knew I wanted to be contacted if my son cut a class or was absent from school for any reason.

CHAPTER 8

A PARENTAL LITERACY DILEMMA

THE RICHARDS FAMILY

Raymond and Tonya Richards and their daughter, Jocelyn, lived on the east side of Bellport. The neighborhood primarily consisted of European Americans who had long-standing ties to Bellport. While there were few African Americans living in this neighborhood, there was a mixture of other races and ethnicities. The Richard's house was a white, split-level ranch with green trim. The lower level held a computer room, where software, educational materials, and other games were available to enhance Jocelyn's literacy experiences at a public school on the east side of the city.

Raymond and Tonya had been married for 7 years. He had a Bachelors of Arts degree in mechanical engineering and was employed in that profession. Tonya was a phlebotomist, with an Associates of Arts degree in applied sciences. The first in their families to complete college, they considered themselves middle class. Tonya and Raymond's parents did not have a college education, but they expected their children to complete college, get good jobs, and live the American dream. Raymond Richards was a member of a fraternity that focused on public service and community involvement; as a result, Mr. and Mrs. Richards were involved in many adult related community activities. They attended religious services at a number of churches, but had not chosen a church home in Bellport.

While attending a fraternity ball, I met Mr. and Mrs. Richards and discovered that their child was a first grade student. During the following week, I contacted them and asked if they would participate in my study of

African American Middle-Income Parents, pages 65–73
Copyright © 2007 by Information Age Publishing
All rights of reproduction in any form reserved.

parental involvement and first grade literacy development. They replied in the affirmative.

The First Meeting

When I rang the doorbell, Jocelyn, a young child with beautiful beaded braids and a pleasant smile, greeted and invited me into the home. She went for her parents as I prepared for the first interview.

As we began our conversation, Mr. Richards asked a multitude of questions related to the media knocking at their door to gather information about middle-class African Americans in the Bellport community. I assured him that this report was confidential.

As we talked, it was revealed that the Richards were not satisfied with the reading progress their daughter had made during the first three months of school. They were very interested in being a part of my study because of this fact.

PARENTAL INVOLVEMENT IN THE HOME

Making Decisions: They Abhorred the Private School Setting

When we met a few weeks later, Mrs. Richards informed me that Jocelyn had attended a private day care center that had been useless in terms of literacy development for their daughter. They blamed the lack of progress on the private school setting, so they decided to enroll her in a public school kindergarten class.

At the first kindergarten parent–teacher conference, the parents discovered that Jocelyn did not recognize some of her lower-case letters and only knew a few numbers. The kindergarten teacher assured them that this was not unusual and Jocelyn would take a little longer to show progress in those areas. The parents were annoyed with the kindergarten teacher's remarks. Mrs. Richards proclaimed,

> We will never send our child to another private school! We'll just keep our $6,000 in our pockets, visit the school frequently, and help her at home. Learning that the child did not know her letters and numbers disturbed me greatly!

As it was revealed, Jocelyn made little progress in kindergarten. Hence, the Richards "shopped around for the best first-grade teacher" at the school. They chose Mrs. Hudson, an African American teacher. "At last we had reached a turning point." Eloquently and happily, Tonya revealed that Mrs. Hudson was more precise about Jocelyn's strengths and weaknesses than the other teachers. At the first parent–teacher conference, Mrs. Hudson told them what they needed to do to help Jocelyn recognize lower-case letters, sounds, and numbers. Mr. Richards said that this eye-opening experience made him and his wife become more involved with their child's education. "We now realize that a delicate task like literacy learning could not be left to the teacher alone; it requires our assistance as well."

Expectations to Raise Literacy Standards: Not Like Déjà Vu

Expectations: Its Impact on the Child's Literacy Learning

The Richards family wanted their daughter to achieve academically. According to Mr. Richards, their responsibility was to ensure the best education for Jocelyn. After talking to the couple about the choice they had made to keep Jocelyn in the neighborhood school, I became interested in knowing what kind of expectations they had set for her and the teacher, Mrs. Hudson.

Raymond expected that Jocelyn's experience with reading would be like déjà vu. On the contrary, her reading progress did not resemble what reading was like for him. He had begun to read at an early age under the tutelage of his mother, who did not have a high school education. Feeling melancholy, Raymond gave details.

> I want her to be much farther ahead in reading. I want her to read! I'm basing it on our schooling. Like I said, the schooling, the abilities that both of us have, she should be reading. At this time of the year when I was in the first grade, I was reading. I did not have what I am able to give to her. Plus, we are helping her; we are involved!

At their first parent–teacher conference, the Richards told Mrs. Hudson what they expected of their daughter in reading. It was their goal that Jocelyn complete level 2a by the end of the school year. Later, I asked about her progress in June, Mrs. Richards stated,

> Jocelyn didn't make the 2a level, but I am pleased because she is at the 1b reading level; she is average. I talked with her teacher the other day after testing and she said Jocelyn had not made the 2a reading level, but she is really trying. She and I have sat and read books that were a little harder than first-grade books. She sounds out words pretty good now. I would like to have had her score a little higher.... Overall, I am pleased with her progress in first-grade. Mrs. Hudson has done a good job teaching Jocelyn to read.

PARENTAL INVOLVEMENT IN THE SCHOOL

Satisfaction: Holding School People in High Esteem

At one of the visits with the Richards, we discussed their satisfaction with Mrs. Hudson, Jocelyn's teacher and the principal, Mrs. Baruba. I wanted to know if Mr. Richards was pleased with the teacher and other school people. When I asked him, this message came through without hesitation. He remarked, "Absolutely! Mrs. Hudson has extended her hours to us; she is at school until 5:30 or 6:00 PM. She encourages us to stop by."

Although Mr. Richards wanted to "visit the classroom more often and maybe speak to the children about his profession as an engineer," he could not do so because of his work schedule. During one of my visits, however, he told me that he took one day away from his job to visit Jocelyn's classroom. He recapped our previous conversation. He stated,

> Remember, I said Jocelyn was having problems learning her letters and numbers earlier during the school year. Well, I took the day off and visited the school during regular school hours just to observe what was being taught and to speak with her teacher about my daughter's progress in reading…. She is improving.

Mr. Richards had a more positive perception of his daughter's public school and also of Mrs. Baruba, the administrator. To illustrate, Mr. Richards shared his thoughts:

> At our second PTO meeting, we did get a chance to talk with the principal of the school. We had met her before, but had not really talked to her in great detail. I was very pleased with her. I like the way she runs the school and her outlook on academic achievement. She spoke about activities that involve students on a multicultural basis. Personally, I feel better knowing that Jocelyn is in a school where she will be exposed to the right type of environment with a diverse population of children.

Effective Communication and Visibility

Not Just a Number to School People
During many meetings, we discussed the Richards' perceptions of involvement and practices with their child's schooling. We explored the topic of communication and visibility within the school. The Richards preferred method of communication was scheduled appointments. Mrs. Richards also stated that another mode of communication was to occasionally visit the principal's office to make sure the office staff knew her, and could connect her to Jocelyn.

Tonya Richards gave details about wanting recognition for Jocelyn, because she did not want their daughter to be just another number in the principal's view. She described an incident that took place in the principal's office.

> Two weeks ago, when I was at the school, I heard the principal, Mrs. Baruba call my daughter Jocelyn by her name, and that just thrilled me. I know I may sound snobbish, but I don't want my child to be treated as if she is a low-income child whose parents don't care about her. Now that the principal knows us, I know that if something happened in the school, Jocelyn wouldn't get lost in the cracks, and that was a goal of mine. I'm hoping that seeing my face at school and knowing Jocelyn by name, will let [the office and lunchroom personnel] know that she has parents who are interested and care about her education.

Tonya believed that visibility assured that their daughter would be treated equitably.

Visibility vis-à-vis School Participation and Excursions

On several occasions, Mrs. Richards indicated that she volunteered at the school. She said,

> I visited the classroom and read stories to the first-grade children. One day when Mrs. Hudson needed another parent to go with them on a field trip, she asked me on the morning that I took Jocelyn to school. Of course, I had to call my job with an excuse about an emergency, before I could commit to chaperoning. Had I not gone on this trip, Jocelyn's class would have missed the excursion to the science museum. Therefore, I went with them; it was a learning experience for me.

Communicating and Socializing With Other Families

Tonya Richards reported that she had participated in several PTO activities. She attended a Meet the Candidates Forum whereby candidates who were running for offices were allowed to speak about their plans and answer questions. Another event the family attended was a movie and popcorn party for the entire family. Of all these activities, Tonya confessed that she enjoyed The Multicultural Fair more than any of the PTO activities, because parents and children from other countries entertained them in song and dance, and of course, "we ate a variety of delicious ethnic foods." Tonya further explained,

> I was on the PTO committee that sponsored that event. As a committee member, I was required to help set up and make desserts for the fair. This was a fund raiser for the school. I was in charge of selling pies, and I also helped with cleanup when the event was over.

Mrs. Richards indicated that participating in this program gave her a better feel for what the PTO did to support the school.

Defending Himself: I'm Not a Deadbeat Father!

African American Fathers' Involvement: The Script Has Flipped

Mr. Richards reported that he saw himself as a provider and head of the household. He believed in being egalitarian in decision-making regarding school placements. He also had recently read an article concerning deadbeat fathers. He refuted "the stereotypical notion that all African American fathers were deadbeats, not living in the home, and did not get involved with their children's schooling." After summarizing the story, Raymond expressed how he was involved with his daughter's education:

> Even though my wife spends more time with her on the fundamentals than I do, I read to her before she goes to bed, but not as much as I would like…. It is a timing problem; I don't get home from work until 7:00 at night. When Jocelyn gets older, I will be the one spending more time with her, helping her with advanced math such as calculus and algebra. I am good in those areas.

Furthermore, he explained,

> I bought Jocelyn a computer program with various levels. It has a phonics program and instructional videos with games. As she progresses, the phonics skill levels change… I sit with her while she uses the computer and direct what she does to make sure she understands.

On a more practical level, how Mr. Richards perceived his involvement and practices with Jocelyn's literacy development is summarized in the following comment:

> One of the things that I have done while traveling was turn off the car radio and have Jocelyn spell rhyming words. We also played rhyming games. When I would take her to day care, there was a code for entering the building. I would say the numbers and watch her punch them in; this was done to increase her memory, self-confidence, and number recognition. At a stop sign, I'd ask her to spell the word "stop." I'd do those things to increase my everyday involvement with her. I have read to Jocelyn, and I've taught her how to use the computer. I also drop her off at school some days and sometimes she takes the bus home.

Mr. Richards revealed that his communications with other males have led him to believe that more fathers are involved with their children's literacy learning and schooling. He said, "this is especially true of African American fathers who have children in early childhood programs."

Homework: The Glue That Connects the Home and School

Near the end of the study, we discussed Jocelyn's progress in reading and math. Both parents agreed that they had seen improvement in their daughter's reading and math development. I asked about homework practices, because I wanted to know if Raymond and Tonya were using the strategies that Mrs. Hudson had shared with them at a parent–teacher conference earlier in the school year. More specifically, I wanted to know what activities had been practiced in the home relative to literacy learning.

Subsequent to learning that their daughter, Jocelyn, was below average in letter and number recognition, the Richards devised their own strategies for dealing with the problems. Mrs. Richards described a typical day:

> As soon as she gets home, we talk about her day, for example, what went on at school. She has a snack, and then we sit and do homework. At first it was sight words and sounds, then math. Now, we are studying consonant blends. Right now, we spend almost an hour and a half on homework every night except weekends.

PARENTAL INVOLVEMENT IN THE COMMUNITY

Child-Related Extracurricular Activities in the Community

Raymond Richards was the primary "provider," yet he also perceived himself as a participant who strategically monitored his daughter's progress. He also stated that he transported Jocelyn to soccer practice during the fall for six weeks and again in the spring. Her age group was not involved in games. He recounted,

> She is only six years old and children that young only practice gaining control of the ball by kicking it. They also learn camaraderie without competition.

When I asked about other extracurricular activities for Jocelyn, Mrs. Richards asserted,

> Jocelyn attends Girl Scouts on Wednesday evenings after school for two hours. She is also taking ballet lessons at Madam Whitaker's dance school on Friday evenings for one hour.

The Richards confessed that their involvement in the community focused only on Jocelyn's activities when they were not involved with Raymond's fraternity programs.

SUMMARY OF A PARENTAL LITERACY DILEMMA

This chapter uncovered the Richards' perceptions of their involvement and practices with their daughter's schooling and the problems she encountered with learning to read. In their effort to find the best teacher for Jocelyn, they networked in the school and chose Mrs. Hudson as Jocelyn's first-grade teacher. She gave them specific literacy suggestions to enhance the child's reading. The parents became visible in the school and developed a collaborative relationship with the teacher and the principal. While Tonya spent more time with Jocelyn's homework than Raymond, he wanted the record to show that he was not a deadbeat father. He was definitely involved and detested how Moynihan's (1965) study on low-income families had painted an unfavorable picture of Black males and that these research findings had been generalized to all Black fathers.

MY PERSONAL REFLECTIONS

As I ponder this family's problem with their daughter's literacy learning, I am reminded of Slaughter-Defoe's (1991) research on private schools. She found that children who attend private schools usually enter public schools well prepared. Raymond and Tonya Richards conveyed their frustration with their daughter's literacy learning in the private sector. I can relate, because as a former teacher, I know of first graders who struggled with reading. On the other hand, my personal recollection is more positive. Why are some children early readers while others are not? Perhaps the answer can be found in my reflections on my own son's early literacy development.

My Son's Literacy Development

As a first-time parent in the 1960's, I taught my son to read. Using a combination of phonics, decoding texts, and literature-based instruction. Consequently, he learned to read before entering kindergarten. Having been a chemist, and an elementary and preschool education teacher, I understood the necessity of early literacy and the positive effect it could have on children's later learning. Did I have all of the answers? No, I did not, but it was my expectation that my son read before he entered kindergarten, because I was an early reader. My parents were not college graduates, and they never finished high school. Yet, they taught all of my siblings to read at an early age. It has been my experience, through dialogue, that many other African Americans grew up in this fashion.

Creating a Partnership With the School: Reflection 1

I can still remember how I created a meaningful partnership with my son's teacher. At that point in time, most teachers did not have teacher assistants in the classroom. As a result, room mothers were a necessity. I immediately became involved as a room mother to help the teacher and to ultimately enhance my child's success. Like the Richards family, I also networked to find the best teacher for him before he entered first grade. Basically, I wanted a teacher who knew how to relate to bright African American boys, and I found that trait in his first-grade teacher.

Creating a Partnership With the School: Reflection 2

Many years ago when Mitchell was in first grade, I was a working Mom. I requested leave from my teaching position to volunteer in his classroom. His teacher always reacted positively toward him, because I made it a point to establish a workable relationship with her at the beginning of the school year (Glenn-Paul, 2000). Sometimes, I would send souvenirs from one of our recent trips. Advocacy was one of my hallmarks; being an advocate for my son was helpful to me as well as him. As he got older, I taught him how to advocate for himself in a suburban school district.

CHAPTER 9

UNCOVERING THE KEY MEANING OF PARENTAL INVOLVEMENT

THE WAYNE FAMILY

Albert and Carrie Wayne lived in the university section of Bellport on a street with a *cul de sac* at the end where children played in relative safety away from traffic. Many of the homes on that street were small colonials. The couple had been married eight years and had two sons. Preston was in prekindergarten and Adrian, the focal child for the study, was a first grader. Both children attended the same public school.

Mr. and Mrs. Wayne came from working-class families. Neither of their parents completed high school. Carrie was the first person in her family to complete college with a Bachelor of Arts degree. She taught a sixth-grade inclusive class while completing her Masters in elementary education and special education at Bellport University. Mr. Wayne had a degree in automotive technology. He was employed as a manager at a car dealership. The Wayne family considered themselves first-generation middle class.

I interviewed the couple at the dining room table, surrounded by an antique china closet, table, and a built-in bookcase filled with a variety of children's books. In addition, there was a bookcase with more children's books in the living room. Some of Carrie's schoolbooks, a lesson planner, and a teacher magazine were on the sofa table. African Art and family photographs hung on the walls of the living room.

African American Middle-Income Parents, pages 75–83
Copyright © 2007 by Information Age Publishing

As a church-going family, Albert and Carrie studied the Bible, weekly, with other young couples from their church, and modeled for their children the religious teachings by which they lived. Mr. Wayne was a deacon in the church and Mrs. Wayne taught Bible school. Their two sons attended Sunday school.

The First Meeting

At my first meeting with the Wayne family, I briefly described my study and asked if they had any questions. Mr. Wayne asked the first question. He inquired, "What do you mean by parent involvement?" My reply was, "parental involvement are those activities that you perceive engaging with your child in the home, at school, and in the community to foster the child's schooling and learning." I tried to keep the explanation very simple, because I did not want them to think I already had the answers to the questions I would ask them during the interviewing process. Ultimately, I wanted to learn from them how they perceived involvement with their first-grade child's education.

Later in the interview, I collected background information about the focal child and the family. This first meeting lasted over an hour, because I had to explain the purpose of the study and the interviewing process. I told Carrie and Albert that I would be interviewing eight intact, African American families, and I needed their participation. They had no idea that the study would last for one year. Carrie told her husband that I would interview them once. Finally, after hearing all that was involved in pursuing a doctoral degree, they agreed to participate in the study.

As I listened to the parents talk, it was my impression that they were involved with their first grader's education, but no one had asked them about their involvement in a structured way. I learned that Adrian was reading at grade level and both parents helped him with homework. When this meeting ended, I asked if I could return for another interview and Albert Wayne said, "Yes." We set up a date and time for another meeting.

PARENTAL INVOLVEMENT IN THE HOME

Soaring Without Choice

Several weeks later, when I visited the Wayne family, I asked Albert and Carrie what had gone on in the area of parent involvement since our last meeting. I merely wanted them to talk freely and openly about their involvement. They told me that both of their children were enrolled at

Madden school. So I asked them why they had chosen to enroll them at Madden school. Carrie responded, "We chose this school because it is convenient. I work there, it's close to home, and the baby-sitter is a couple of blocks away." As relayed, the Wayne's sons attended the neighborhood school for reasons different from any of the other children in this book who attended either private or public schools.

Reading: A Nightly Ritual

Albert also reported that as a ritual, he read to the children at bedtime. He felt it was their responsibility to teach their sons. "You have got to teach them, not just educationally, but spiritually too. Teach them to read the Bible." Mrs. Wayne added to the conversation and said,

> Yesterday Adrian got a new Bible and he read about *Jesus in the Temple.* I had to help him with some of the words, but he knew the three and four letter words. He sounded them out. It was really refreshing to see him sound out words.

Carrie also mentioned helping with homework. She stated,

> One of us helps with homework every night. He has six different spelling words (e.g., may, say, day, throw, some, and fun) every week and he does great on the tests. I just went over the words with him because he has a test tomorrow.

Now the Teacher Knows Our Expectations

Expectations for the Teacher

On another occasion, when I visited the Waynes, we discussed setting expectations. I wanted to know what expectations Albert and Carrie had set for their son and Mrs. McNeilly, his first-grade teacher.

Mrs. Wayne told an interesting story about pursuing more challenging schoolwork for him. She said,

> Adrian is doing great in school. He is above level in reading, but he needs to be challenged more in math. Nevertheless, we try to take care of that at home. We give him little assignments to complete. Last year, the teacher gave him some math sheets and we worked with him at home. I have talked with Mrs. McNeilly about challenging him more in math. Now she knows what we expect.

Mr. Wayne echoed a similar response when he expressed his expectations of his son's teacher. He responded,

I expect the teacher to let us know if Adrian is falling down in an area. She can tell us where he is slipping and help him get back on level. We will work in conjunction with her to get him back on level. I would also expect materials, phone calls, and anything that could help us to enhance his learning. I think that's her job!

Expectations for the Child

Albert Wayne also reported his perspective of the expectations they desired for Adrian. He said,

We tell Adrian that it is very important to learn to read and write and get a good education, because when he gets older and goes into the job market...he will need good skills. He will need to be marketable to get a good job. We teach him to... finish high school and go to college. We also tell him that if he wants to get nice things, he will need money.

PARENTAL INVOLVEMENT IN THE SCHOOL

Awareness of School Activities: PTO Involvement

As we continued to meet, the parents were more open when we discussed school involvement roles. At this particular meeting, I began our interview by asking, "What has the school done to involve you in your son's education?" It was revealed that Albert had been asked to participate in a school-wide activity. He explained,

Mrs. McNeilly, Adrian's teacher, asked me if I would play Santa Claus for the holiday program. She brought her father's Santa costume to school for me. Attending and participating in the holiday program was the only parent involvement activity we did in December, other than helping Adrian with homework assignments and monitoring how his schooling had gone.

Carrie indicated that December was one of the busiest months of the year, but they arranged their schedules so that they could be involved with school activities for the sake of their children.

During another conversation, Mr. Wayne informed me that he had been involved in the PTO's rummage sale. The PTO president called him to volunteer after seeing his name on the sign-up list handed out at the first PTO meeting:

At the first PTO meeting, we filled out a card saying that we would be able to volunteer sometimes. So, the PTO president called me to work at the rummage sale. I did not have to work all day. I picked the time slot that I would be available and worked for two hours one Saturday.

As the year progressed, Albert and Carrie continued to report their involvement with Adrian's schooling. Carrie described,

Although we knew how well Adrian was performing academically, we made an appointment to attend our second parent–teacher conference. Mrs. McNeilly assured us that he was continuing to make progress in reading and math.

Albert expressed his perspective on their school involvement.

In February, we attended a Black History Program. It was a potluck dinner and the children entertained us. Each class had a presentation, and most of the teachers were dressed in African clothing.

Since Carrie was a teacher at Madden school, she was well aware of Adrian's assignments. On one occasion, she explained the morning classroom routine. Her descriptions of the classroom activities were as vivid as a picture on a digital camera. Her explanation caused me to believe that she had spent some time observing in her son's classroom. As previously conveyed, she and her husband helped Adrian with homework, especially with math, reading, and spelling.

Other ways that Carrie was involved at the school included taking personal days from work to chaperone Adrian's class on field trips. She recounted,

I went with Adrian's class on a walking trip to the public library to get library cards and check out books. Only the children who already had cards could withdraw books. There were three adults—two teachers and I. Each of us was responsible for a small group of kids. Next month, they will be going to the science museum. I can't go, because my class will be taking fourth grade tests. However, I plan to go with them on a camping trip in June.

Teacher Satisfaction: She Gave Us Her Telephone Number

Mr. and Mrs. Wayne had established a positive rapport with Mrs. McNeilly when their son was enrolled in her kindergarten class. Albert and Carrie stated their satisfaction with the teacher in a very positive manner:

We are very satisfied with Mrs. McNeilly. She taught our son Adrian in kindergarten. Now she has him for first grade. She is looping [or she teaches the same children for two consecutive years]. When we spoke with her at open house in September, she even gave us her home telephone number. I was impressed that she would give us her home number.

Mrs. Wayne articulated her feelings:

You know what I really like about her? When Adrian started out in kindergarten, she made a visit to our house before school started and took pictures of him. She said, 'Hi' to him. He was shy. It wasn't a visit for us to sit down and talk. It was for Adrian. She didn't have to make that clear verbally, but physically we could tell that the visit was for him. She took his picture. All of the pictures of her students were placed on a bulletin board in her classroom.

Silent Communication: Visibility and the School's Newsletter

As I listened to Albert and Carrie dialogue about their methods of communicating with their son's teacher, I realized their responses were focused on the schools' mode of communication with the home through the school's newsletter. Mr. Wayne described Madden's school newsletter as a communication tool:

We get a newsletter from the school inviting us to participate in various activities. I have tried to keep up with the newsletter after you asked me about the events that were going on at the school. We get things like field trip permission notes, PTO information, budget updates, and upcoming events.

Mrs. Wayne, who was also pleased with the school's newsletter, expressed satisfaction in the following quote:

I view the newsletter as an invitation to get parents involved. Sometimes they send home parent/child family books. Recently, they sent us a sheet that included tips for the summer. It was about continuing to educate or teach your child during the summer. It had some good tips and activities about how to make teachable moments in everything that you do with your child. I really liked it!

Although Mrs. Wayne had the opportunity to communicate with Adrian's teacher, daily, she was not intrusive; neither did she visit the classroom without an established appointment. While she had Mrs. McNeilly's telephone number, she only called her during an emergency situation.

Reflecting on Literacy Activities: I Didn't Know He Could Write

In contrast to some of the parents in this book whose children were having a slow beginning with literacy learning, Albert and Carrie testified that Adrian was a reader and writer. They were excited that he wanted to participate in the Black History Essay writing contest. He wrote his essay at home and submitted it to Mrs. McNeilly, his teacher. She entered it in the contest, and he won first place. This contest was for students in kindergarten through sixth-grade. To assist him, Mrs. Wayne used the videotape, *My Friend Martin*. She expressed her excitement:

> It's a cartoon, but it is done with various Black actors and actresses. Whoopi Goldberg and Oprah Winfrey, everybody is in it! He viewed that tape and he read a couple of books that we have at home; then he was ready to write his story.

Mr. Wayne, who was also excited with Adrian's achievement, said,

> I was shocked! When you (interviewer) told us that first graders could write, I didn't understand, but now I do. Adrian was happy that he had won. I like to see the excitement in his eyes. At first, I thought he had won it for his first-grade class, but the whole school (K–6) was involved. It was good, but kind of sad that others (e.g., older students) did not participate. What happened to the sixth graders?

PARENTAL INVOLVEMENT
THROUGH CHURCH AND COMMUNITY

When I asked about their parental involvement roles in the community, Mr. Wayne explained,

> We are members of an Interdenominational Religious Church. We attend Bible study during the week, and we're also actively involved in other church activities. Our sons are also involved in children's ministry. With regard to community involvement beyond the church, Mrs. Wayne interjected, "I am a Board member of Healthy Start, a program designed to help women have healthy pregnancies and positive birth outcomes. The program meets monthly and also deals with young children's health issues."

Mr. Wayne admitted that at our first interview when I asked them about parental involvement, he did not understand that it could be defined so broadly. At the end of our interviews, he summed up what it meant to him as a middle-income African parent as follows:

> Parental involvement could entail helping with homework, picking up children from school, or communicating with the teacher about the child's progress. Another parent might serve on the school board; that parent is still involved, but in a different way. Now I realize that parent involvement can be a wide range of activities. It really depends on how much parents want to get involved. We could do the whole gamut or only do what fits us.

SUMMARY OF UNCOVERING
THE MEANING OF INVOLVEMENT

In this chapter there emerged parents' perceptions of involvement and practices with their son, Adrian's education. Albert and Carrie Wayne enrolled Adrian at Madden, the neighborhood school, because it was convenient. In addition, Mrs. Wayne was a teacher at the school; it was close to home, and the day care provider lived in the neighborhood. Albert revealed his involvement with the PTO. Carrie communicated with the child's teacher, and volunteered in school activities. In the home, both parents assisted Adrian with his homework, read to him, and listened to him read the Bible. Interestingly, Adrian won first place in the Black History Essay Contest; he wrote about Dr. Martin Luther King Jr.'s contributions to the American people. The parents were ecstatic to see him win. According to Carrie, because their son was reading above grade level, his literacy understanding influenced his writing success.

MY PERSONAL REFLECTIONS

As I contemplate what it was like teaching my son at home before he entered kindergarten, I cannot minimize the significance of my accomplishments. However, I often wonder how it would have been if he had not learned alphabet/letter-sound correspondences at an early age? The answer is simple, he would have a reading problem today. To prepare him to read, I stressed phonemic awareness, because it is the key to reading and understanding what is conveyed in a passage (Adams, 1990; National Reading Panel, 2000). I also used literature-based instruction to teach him how to read.

My Son's Literacy Development

Like Mrs. Wayne, I also taught at the same school that my son attended when he was a first grader. I, too, was careful about when and how I communicated with his teacher during school time. I always made an appointment whenever I needed to talk with her about his progress. One time, at the end of the marking period, Mitchell was given a lower grade in math than we expected. We made an appointment to meet with his teacher. At that meeting, we discussed his grade and requested that he be tested. After testing, Mitchell's score revealed that he was functioning at a higher level. Therefore, his grade was changed. My son, like Mrs. Wayne's son, was also an early reader. The reason being, "I primed the pump" in the early years, and helped him develop phonemic awareness before he entered kindergarten.

In chapter 10, I present the conclusion of parental responses to their perceived involvement and practices with their first-grade children's education and schooling.

CONCLUSION

Parents' comments suggest that being in the middle-income bracket provides an opportunity for them to actively pursue involvement in home and school activities and allows them to make every attempt to ensure their child's welfare in the school environment. This is in contrast to the picture that popular media and the news have presented regarding middle-income African American families.

Researchers cannot make inferences about one population based on findings for another. However, studies that have focused on low-income African American parents have generalized to middle-income African Americans, suggesting that all African Americans (regardless of income) are uninvolved with their children's education (Hannerz, 1969; Peters, 1974; Slaughter & Epps, 1987).

Acquiring an understanding of middle-income, African American families' involvement is important, because few studies have given attention to their participation and practices with first graders. Thus, current comments elicited from these eight intact middle-income, African American families extends past research on parental involvement by identifying themes that have different indications of what parent involvement means to them.

Based on parents' perceptions of their involvement and reported practices, the middle-income, African American families in this book revealed how they were engaged with their first-grade children's education in traditional and nontraditional ways. For example, several aspects of the discourse in the traditional context were parent and educator interactions, such as parent–teacher conferences, open houses, and PTO meetings. Some families participated in these events. In the home context, they reported sharing bedtime stories, and helping with homework and school related tasks. In essence, homework was like the cement that kept the home and school connected.

In addition, the nontraditional discourse consisted of home experiences that provided some children with participation and exposure to the latest computer software, spiritual stories, study skills, environmental print, and recreational reading.

In an effort to prepare their children for the future, some parents expressed their desires and aspirations for them and used *participatory practices* to stress the notion of attaining good grades. The term participatory practices was coined from *anticipatory socialization,* (Scanzoni, 1971). In his study on Black families above the poverty level, Scanzoni's explanation of the term anticipatory socialization was a method of counsel and example used by Black parents to help their children get ahead in life. In a related vein, participatory practices, stressed by the parents in this book, emphasized futuristic practices such as, finishing high school, completing college, becoming employed in salaried positions, and living the American dream. Certainly, some participatory practices were accomplished immediately and involved home experiences such as, story time, educational video games, toys, and popular television characters (e.g., Dora, Barney, Bob the Builder, and Elmo), that taught literacy and mathematical computations to enhance children's learning.

Some parents engaged their children in intangible and futuristic experiences such as visiting and discussing college campuses. To develop the social, spiritual, and aesthetic domains, some parents promoted community-based family focused activities (i.e., visiting friends, attending church functions, visiting the library, and participating in music, dance, and concerts). Among these middle-income African American families, the functional value of these experiences was to increase children's spiritual, physical, cultural, and academic development. Ultimately, they wanted their children to be well rounded and believed that extra curricular activities and out of school experiences would help in that domain.

In conclusion, these eight intact middle-income, African American families were economically secure, stable, and supportive in every aspect of their children's lives. Their perceptions of their involvement and reported practices were the necessary elements for school success. Finally, the level of involvement and reported practices did not differ significantly among spouses. But a significant aspect for the African American community is that the fathers in this book embraced their egalitarian roles and this factor seemed to predict the quality and quantity of school and home involvement.

REFERENCES

American Fact Finder U.S. Census Bureau. (1999). Available at http://uup.csuohio .edu/publications/entire.pdf.

Adams, M. J. (1990). *Beginning to read: Thinking and learning about print.* Cambridge, MA: MIT Press.

Allington, R., & Cunningham, P. (2002). *Schools that work: Where all children read and write.* Boston: Allyn & Bacon.

Attewell, P., Lavin, D., Thurston, D., & Levy, T., (2004, Summer-Fall). The Black middle class: Progress, prospects and puzzles. *Journal of African American Studies, 8*(1), 6–19.

Bandura, A. (1997). *Self efficacy: The exercise of control.* New York: Freeman.

Bandura, A., Barbaranelli, C., Caprara, G. V., & Pastorelli, C. (1996). Multifaceted-impact of self-efficacy beliefs on academic functioning. *Child Development, 67,* 1206–1222.

Baumann, J. F., & Thomas, D. (1999). If you can pass momma's tests, then she knows you're getting your education: A case study of support for literacy learning within an African American family. *The Reading Teacher, 51,* 108–120.

Billingsley, A. (1992). *Climbing Jacob's ladder: The enduring legacy of African American families.* New York: Simon and Schuster.

Blachman, B. A. (1998, September). *Learning disabilities: A focus on early intervention.* Paper presented at the Syracuse University Semi Centennial Conference on Literacy, Syracuse, NY.

Bogdan, R., & Biklen, S. K. (1998). *Qualitative research for education: An introduction to theory and methods* (3rd ed.). Boston: Allyn and Bacon.

Bronfenbrenner, U. (1974). *A report on longitudinal evaluations of preschool programs, (Vol. II): Is early intervention effective?* Office of Child Development, U.S. Department of Health Education, and Welfare. (ERIC Document Reproduction of Service No. ED093501)

Comer, J. P. (1986). Parent participation in the school. *Phi Delta Kappan, 67,* 442–446.

Comer, J. P. (November 1988). Educating poor minority children. *Scientific American, 259*(5), 42–48.

African American Middle-Income Parents, pages 87–90
Copyright © 2007 by Information Age Publishing

Comer, J. P., & Haynes, N. M. (1991). Parent involvement in schools: An ecological approach. *The Elementary School Journal, 91,* 271–277.

Coner-Edwards, A. F., & Spurlock, J. (1988). *Black families in crisis: The middle class.* New York: The Free Press.

Cose, E. (1993). *The rage of a privileged class.* NY: Harper Collins Publishers.

Cose, E. (1999, June 7). The good news about Black America. *Newsweek, 133,* 28–40.

Coupland, D. (1991). *Generation X: Tales for an accelerated culture.* New York: St. Martins Press.

Dauber, S. L., & Epstein, J. L., (1993). Parents' attitudes and practices of involvement in inner-city elementary and middle schools. In N. F. Chavkin (Ed.), *Families and school in a pluralistic society* (pp. 53–71). Albany, NY: State University of New York Press.

Delgado-Gaitan, C. (1992). School matters in the Mexican American home: Socializing children to education. *American Educational Research Journal, 29*(3), 495–513.

Delpit, L. (1988). The silenced dialogue: Power and pedagogy in educating other people's children. *Harvard Educational Review, 58,* 280–298.

Drum Major Institute. (June 2004). The middle-class squeeze: An overview. [Online] http://www.themiddleclass.org

Eccles, J. S., & Harold, R. D. (1993). Parent–school involvement during the early adolescent years. *Teachers College Record, 94,* 568–586.

Edwards, P. A. (1995). Combining parents' and teachers' thoughts about storybooks at home and school. In L. M. Morrow (Ed.), *Family literacy: Multiple perspectives to enhance literacy development* (pp. 54–60). Newark, DE: International Reading Association.

Edwards, P. A. (2004). *Children's literacy development.* Boston: Pearson.

Epstein, J. L. (1991a). Effects on student achievement of teachers' practices of parent involvement. In S. B. Silvern (Ed.), *Advances in reading/language research: Vol. 5. Literacy through family, community, and school interaction* (pp. 261–276). Greenwich, CT: JAI Press.

Epstein, J. L. (1996). Perspectives and previews on research and policy for school, family, and community partnerships. In A. Booth & J. Dunn (Eds.), *Family-school links: How do they affect educational outcomes?* (pp. 209–246). New Jersey: Lawrence Erlbaum Associates.

Espinosa, L. M. (1995). *Hispanic parent involvement in early programs.* Urbana, IL: University of Illinois, ERIC/EECE Publication. (ERIC Document Reproduction Service No. PS955)

Fine, M. (1993, Spring). A parent's involvement. *Equity and Choice, 9*(3), 4–8.

Galper, A., Wigfield, A., & Seefeldt, C. (1997). Head start parents' beliefs about their children's abilities, task, values, and performances on different activities. *Child Development, 68,* 897–907.

Glenn-Paul, D. (2000). Rap and orality: Critical media literacy, pedagogy, and cultural synchronization. *Journal of Adolescent & Adult Literature, 44*(3), 246–251.

Hannerz, U. (1969). *Soulside: Inquiries into ghetto culture and community.* New York: Columbia University Press.

Heath, S. B. (1983). *Ways with words: Language, life and work in communities and classrooms.* Cambridge, MA: Cambridge University Press.

Henderson, A. T. (1987). *The evidence continues to grow. Parent Involvement improves student achievement.* Washington, DC: National Committee for Citizens in Education.

Henderson, A. T., & Berla, N. (1994). *A new generation of evidence: The family is critical to student achievement.* Washington, DC: National Committee for citizens in Education International Development Research Association (IDRA), (1988) San Antonia, TX.

Hoover-Dempsey, K. V., & Sandler, H. M. (1997, Spring). Why do parents become involved in their children's education? *Review of Educational Research, 67*(1), 3–42.

Klein, A. (2004, December 18). A tenuous hold on the middle class: African Americans on shifting ground. *The Washington Post.* Retrieved February 23, 2005, from http://www.washingtonpost.com

Kvale, S. (1996). *InterViews: An introduction to qualitative research interviewing.* Thousand Oaks, CA: Sage Publications.

Lamb, M. (1997). *The role of the father in child development* (3rd ed.), New York: John Wiley & Sons.

Lightfoot, S. L. (1978). *Worlds Apart: Relationships between families and schools.* New York: Basic Books.

Masci, D. (1998). The Black middle class: Is its cup half-full or half empty? *Congressional Quarterly Researcher. 8*(13), 49–72.

McAdoo, H. P. (1997). Upward mobility across generations in African American families. In H. P. McAdoo (Ed.), *Black families* (3rd ed., pp.139–162). Thousand Oaks, CA: Sage Publications Inc.

McAdoo, J. L. (1997). The roles of African American fathers in the socialization of their children. In H. P. McAdoo. (Ed.), *Black families* (3rd ed., pp. 183–197). Thousand Oaks, CA: Sage Publications Inc.

Moynihan, D. P. (1965). *The Negro family: A case for national action.* Washington, DC: Department of Labor, Office of Policy Planning and Research.

National Institute of Child Health and Human Development. (2000). *Report of the National Reading Panel: Teaching children to read: An evidence-based assessment of the scientific research on reading and its implications for reading instruction. Reports of the Subgroups.* Washington, DC: U.S. Government Printing Office.

National Reading Panel. (2000). http://www.nationalreadingpanel.org/default.htm.

No Child Left Behind Act of 2001, Pub. L. No. 107–110, § 1201, 115 Stat. 1535. (2002). Retrieved May 29, 2002, from http://edworkforce.house.gov/issues/107th/education/nclb/nclb.htm

Ogbu, J. U. (1977). Racial stratification and education: The case of Stockton, California. *IRCD Bulletin, 12*(3), 1–26.

Ogbu, J. U. (1995). Literacy and Black Americans: Comparative perspectives. In V. Gadsden & D. Wagner (Eds.), *Literacy among African American youth: Issues in learning, teaching, and schooling* (pp. 83–100). Cresskill, NJ: Hampton Press.

Ortiz, R., S. Stile, & Brown, C. (1999). Early Literacy activities of fathers: Reading and writing with young children. *Young Children, 54*(5),16–18.

Overstreet, S., Devine, J., Bevans, K., & Efreom, Y. (2005). Predicting parental involvement in children's schooling within an economically disadvantaged African American sample. *Psychology in the Schools. 42*(1), 101–111.

Paul, D. G. (2000). *Raising Black children who love reading and writing: A guide from birth through grade six.* Westport, CT: Bergin & Garvey.

Peters, M. F. (1974, October). The Black family: Perpetuating the myths—An analysis of family: Sociological textbook treatment of Black families. *Family Coordinator, 23*, 349–57.

Peters, M. F. (1981). *Child rearing in Black families: Potential continuities and discontinuities between home and school.* Paper presented at annual meeting of National Council on Family Relations, Portland, OR.

Rich, D. (1988). *Megaskills: How families can help children succeed in school and beyond.* Boston: Houghton Mifflin Company.

Reed, R. P., Jones, K. P., Walker, J. M., & Hoover-Dempsey, K. V. (2000, April). *Parents' motivation for involvement in children's education: Testing a theoretical model.* Paper presented at the annual meeting of the American Educational Research Association, New Orleans.

Robinson, E. S. (1999). *How do African American parents perceive and participate in their children's literacy learning activities in the home?* Unpublished research apprenticeship report. Syracuse, NY: Syracuse University.

Sadoski, M., & Willson, V. L. (2006). Effects of a theoretically based large-scale reading intervention in a multicultural urban school district. *American Educational Research Journal, 43*, 137–154.

Scanzoni, J. H. (1971). *The Black family in modern society.* Boston: Allyn and Bacon.

Schmidt, P. R. (1998). The abc's of cultural understanding and communication. *Equity and Excellence in Education, 31*(2), 28–38.

Schmidt, P. R. (2005). *Preparing teachers to communicate and connect with families and communities.* Greenwich, CT: Information Age Publishing.

Schutz, A. (1970). *On phenomenology and social relations.* Chicago: University of Chicago.

Seefeldt, C., Denton, K., Galper, A., & Younoszai, T. (1998). Former Head Start parents characteristics, perceptions of school climate, and involvement in their children's education. *The Elementary School Journal, 98*, 339–349.

Seidman, I. E. (1998). *Interviewing as qualitative research: A guide for researchers in education and the social sciences* (2nd Ed.). New York: Teachers College Press.

Sheldon, S. B. (2002) Parents' school networks and beliefs as predictors of parent involvement. *The Elementary School Journal, 102*(4), 301–316.

Slaughter, D. T., & Epps, E. G. (1987). The home environment and academic achievement of Black American children and youth: An overview. *The Journal of Negro Education, 56*(1), 3–20.

Slaughter-Defoe, D. T. (1991). Parental educational choice: Some African American dilemmas. *Journal of Negro Education, 60*, 354–360.

Stake, R. E. (1995*). The art of case study research.* Thousand Oaks, CA: Sage Publications.

Stake, R. E. (2000). Case studies. In N. K. Denzin & W. S. Lincoln (Eds.), *Handbook of qualitative research* (2nd ed., pp. 435–454). Thousand Oaks, CA: Sage Publications.

Taylor, D. &, Dorsey-Gaines, C. (1988). *Growing up literate: Learning from inner city families.* Portsmouth, NH: Heinemann.

U.S. Department of Education. (1994). *Goals 2000: Educate america act legislative* Summary Author.

U.S. Department of Education. (1994). *Strong families strong schools: Building community partnerships for learning.* Washington, DC: Author.

Yin, R. K. (1994). *Case study research: Design and methods* (2nd ed.). Applied Social Research Methods Series: Sage Publications.

ABOUT THE AUTHOR

Ethel Swindell Robinson received her Ph.D. in Reading Education from Syracuse University. She is currently owner of Swindell Associates, a Family Literacy Consulting Firm. Her areas of interest are religious education, family literacy, early education, and parental involvement. Dr. Swindell Robinson is the past recipient of two Women of Achievement Awards in education. One is from the Syracuse Alumnae Chapter of Delta Sigma Theta Sorority in 1977, and the other was awarded by the Post Standard Newspaper in 1987.

African American Middle-Income Parents, page 91
Copyright © 2007 by Information Age Publishing

Printed in the United States
98149LV00001B/262-315/A

9 781593 118297